ROCK CLIMBING

Phil Watts, PhD
Northern Michigan University

Library of Congress Cataloging-in-Publication Data

Watts, Phillip Baxter, 1951-
Rock climbing / Phil Watts.
p. cm. -- (Outdoor pursuits series)
Includes index.
ISBN 0-87322-814-6
1. Rock climbing. I. Title. II. Series.
GV200.2.W38 1996
796.5'223--dc20 95-38817
CIP

ISBN: 0-87322-814-6

An important note to readers: This is an instructional book about rock climbing, a sport that is potentially dangerous. Because of the risks involved in rock climbing, the author and publisher strongly recommend that the information provided in this book be used only to supplement qualified personal instruction from a climbing expert or guide.

Developmental Editor: Julie Rhoda; **Assistant Editors:** Susan Moore, Kirby Mittelmeier, Ann Greenseth, John Wentworth, Sandra Merz Bott; **Editorial Assistant:** Jennifer Hemphill; **Copyeditor:** Michael Ryder; **Proofreader:** Jim Burns; **Indexer:** Barbara E. Cohen; **Typesetters:** Stuart Cartwright and Ruby Zimmerman; **Text Designer:** Keith Blomberg; **Layout Artist:** Stuart Cartwright; **Photo Editor:** Boyd LaFoon; **Photographer (interior):** Richard Etchberger, unless otherwise noted; **Photographer (cover):** Daniel Levison/Vertical Imagery; **Cover Designer:** Jack Davis; **Illustrator:** Thomas • Bradley Illustration & Design

Printed in Hong Kong 10 9 8 7 6 5 4 3 2 1

Human Kinetics
P.O. Box 5076, Champaign, IL 61825-5076
1-800-747-4457

Canada: Human Kinetics, Box 24040, Windsor, ON N8Y 4Y9
1-800-465-7301 (in Canada only)

Europe: Human Kinetics, P.O. Box IW14, Leeds LS16 6TR, United Kingdom
(44) 1132 781708

Australia: Human Kinetics, 2 Ingrid Street, Clapham 5062, South Australia
(08) 371 3755

New Zealand: Human Kinetics, P.O. Box 105-231, Auckland 1
(09) 523 3462

CONTENTS

1

GOING ROCK CLIMBING

The Sierra sky is a perfect blue and, although it is midsummer, the morning air is comfortably cool as you move upward. Your hands search for bumps and knobs in and around the single crack that wanders up this white granite slab. There is a joy in your movements—a lightness expressed as subtle balances, gentle pulls, and precise steps—as you follow an ancient fissure. The lake, some 300 vertical feet below, promises a relaxing swim once the summit is attained and a careful descent is negotiated. For now, it's just the sun, the wind, and the movement over the rock. This is rock climbing at its best—high and free in a beautiful, natural environment.

Mountain summits have figured significantly in history since Moses' early trek up Mt. Sinai and the Emperor Hadrian's 2nd-century A.D. ascent of Mount Etna to view the sunrise. In the early 18th century, the glacier-clad Alps of Europe began to attract a few adventurers and scientists, and by the 1850s recreational mountaineering was well established and the first climbing club had been formed.

As the easier summits were attained and attention turned toward more difficult peaks, it became necessary to develop safety equipment and master specialized skills for climbing rock. Even into the early 20th century, difficult rock climbing was considered to be mere practice for ascending the world's high peaks. Since the 1930s, however, rock climbing has evolved into a great outdoor activity in its own right. Today, climbers of all ages enjoy routes up easy, low-angled slabs, steep, vertical faces, and difficult, nearly horizontal, overhangs.

Rock climbing has been described as dance-like, even playful, like a game. Climbs vary from short traverses just inches off the ground to continuous ascents of soaring walls that involve thousands of dizzying feet. You can join in at whatever level is comfortable for you.

Thin crack climbing in Tuolumne Meadows, California.

Why Rock Climbing?

One attraction of rock climbing is the opportunity for personal challenge. Climbing routes are rated for difficulty on an ascending numerical scale that enables you to follow your progress and select new challenges as former ones are achieved.

As a social activity, climbing is hard to beat. Families and friends can gather at the crag for a day of routes, then casually reminisce around the evening campfire. The natural setting of most rock-climbing areas provides you with opportunities to combine climbing with other outdoor activities, like mountain biking up the Owens River Gorge in California or backpacking into the Enchantment Lakes wilderness of Washington.

The various types of rock yield different textures and features. These produce different "moods" of climbing, from the powerful, steep quartzite cranking at Devil's Lake in Wisconsin to the delicate balance and precise footwork required on the glacier-polished granite of Tuolumne Meadows in California. Learning to recognize and use these features as hand- and footholds provides an intriguing element of problem solving in rock climbing.

ROCK FEATURES

arete—A sharp, outside corner of rock.
buckets—Large holds with positive lips.
buttress—A major corner feature; larger than an arete.
chimney—A crack big enough to fit most or all of the body into.
crimpers—Small yet positive edges of rock, just big enough for the fingertips to grip or smaller.
dihedral—An inside corner of rock. Also known as an "open book."
edges—Small ledges of rock of various sizes.
face—A steep, flat expanse of rock.
flake—A wafer-like section of rock that has peeled part way from the main face. Flakes can be as small as single handholds or big enough to crawl behind.
horn—A "horn-like" projection of rock, usually grasped at the top.
jug—A projection or column of rock that is grasped like a jug handle.
knobs—Projections of rock that are grasped or pinched with the fingers or hand. Knobs are often crystals imbedded in the main rock.
niche—A pocket or alcove in the rock that is at least large enough for both hands or both feet. When a niche is big enough for one's entire body, it is often called an alcove.
overhang—A rock feature that is steeper than vertical.
pockets—Holes or dimples in the rock. A big pocket can be a bucket.
ramp—A ledge-like feature that leads upward and across the main rock.
roof—A large, horizontal overhang. Also called a ceiling.
slab—A low, angled, relatively smooth sheet of rock.

One of the major benefits of rock climbing is its contribution to overall physical fitness. The available range of difficulties enables almost anyone to begin climbing, and continuing the activity gradually develops one's strength, endurance, flexibility, and balance. Perhaps best of all, rock climbing leads to summits—the elusive high places of dreams and visions.

Types of Rock Climbing

Advances in equipment and techniques have made the sport available and relatively safe for persons of all ages. Modern nylon climbing ropes are virtually unbreakable when used appropriately, and new anchor devices have simplified overall protection for the climber.

Bouldering provides energetic practice for a solitary climber or problem-solving challenges among friends.

The most basic form of rock climbing is *bouldering*, or climbing over rock close to the ground without anchors, ropes, and harnesses. Easy to very difficult movements may be tried in relative safety, particularly if a partner *spots,* or helps to catch the climber during short falls. The purity of bouldering appeals to many: Except for a pair of specialized rock shoes and a bit of gymnastic chalk for the fingers, it's just you and the rock.

When the rock gets high enough that serious injury or death could result from a fall, most climbers use a rope and an anchor system. The *anchor system* consists of one or more solid points of attachment of the rope to the rock. Anchors may be natural features, such as trees or rock horns, or mechanical devices, which the climber carries and wedges into the rock. One end of the rope is tied through a harness worn around the climber's waist and attached to the anchors by spring-gated, aluminum carabiners. The other end of the rope is managed by the climber's partner, who can apply a braking force that enables the rope and anchor system to hold, or catch, a fallen climber.

Many smaller crags can be top-roped to provide a wide safety margin.

Often, a convenient trail provides access to the top of a rock crag. In such cases, an anchor system for the rope may be set up at the top of the crag before climbing begins and the route *top-roped.*

Sometimes there is no easy route, and you must lead the rope as you climb by setting intermediate anchors along the way. These intermediate anchors are established at intervals along the climbing route, and the rope clipped onto each anchor using a carabiner. This practice limits falls to the distance between the climber and her last anchor plus that distance again as the fall continues past the anchor and the rope tightens.

The two types of leading differ in how the intermediate anchors are established. *Traditional leads* involve the climber configuring anchor points in the rock during the ascent using an assortment of devices, or protection (*pro* for short), which are carried on a cord around the neck or on the climber's harness. The pro is recovered by the leader's partner, the *second*, as she follows the route.

Making decisions about where and how to place protection adds to the challenge of traditional leading.

The second type, *sport leads*, involve the use of preset anchors, usually steel bolts, that have been permanently fixed along the route. These anchors normally are spaced such that falls will be relatively short and the climber can concentrate on solving the movement complexities of the route. For this reason, sport routes tend to be difficult.

With bolt anchors in place, sport leading is often called "clip and go" climbing.

Both types of leading involve more than merely making the moves on the rock. The leader must continually make decisions regarding the direction of the route, when and how to place solid intermediate anchors, and how best to conserve energy. Leading rock climbs is serious business: It requires a steady mind and body and the experience necessary to make appropriate judgments.

Difficulty Ratings for Rock Climbs

Once you have mastered the basics of rock climbing, you can evaluate your progress by attempting more difficult routes. Published guidebooks that describe specific routes are often available for established climbing areas. The general difficulty of a particular route is assigned a numerical "Class" value:

- Class 1— walking over relatively flat terrain.
- Class 2—hiking over varied terrain on trails or through open country.
- Class 3—scrambling over steep terrain where the hands are occasionally used for balance and support. Be careful with the term *Class 3*, however; it doesn't always mean the climbing is easy. Some guidebooks use the term to indicate climbing unroped, regardless of the difficulty.
- Class 4—climbing over easy terrain requiring significant use of the hands and arms for support and where a fall could be fatal. Many climbers will put on a harness, tie into the rope, and use anchors on Class-4 routes.
- Class 5—technical climbing where a rope, anchors, and other specialized equipment are always used for protection. Class-5 climbing, also known as *free climbing*, is the primary focus of this text. The term *free climbing* here is not to be confused with *free soloing*, which means climbing technical Class-5 rock without a rope (as you would in Class-3 climbing)—a very dangerous proposition.
- Class 6—climbing that requires the use of artificial means such as pulling on the rope, standing on devices placed in the rock, or ascending some type of ladder. Class-6 climbing is often referred to as *aid climbing* and is designated by the letter *A* followed by a number, from 0 to 5, to indicate the overall difficulty level.

Subjective systems have been developed around the world to rate the difficulty of various Class-5 rock climbs. The Yosemite Decimal System (YDS) is most common for North American routes and currently ranges from 5.0 through 5.14d. Such ratings can help you discriminate among several potential routes and give you some idea whether a route is appropriate for a novice, or is one that would scare him out of the sport forever. These numerical systems also enable you to note your personal progress in climbing.

It is important to realize, however, that all of the rating systems are subjective. A particular climb may actually "feel" quite different to different persons. Traditionally, the rating has indicated the difficulty of the hardest

ROCK-CLIMBING RATING SYSTEMS			
American	**French**	**Australian**	**Likely perception**
5.0-5.4 5.5-5.6		10-11 12-13	Straightforward moves with variable size holds.
5.7 5.8 5.9	5a 5b 5c	14-15 16 17	More complex moves and positions over steeper terrain with smaller hand and foot holds.
5.10a 5.10b 5.10c 5.10d	6a 6b	18 19 20 21	A hand- and/or foothold may be missing for some moves. May require some specific training yet is "do-able" by mere mortals.
5.11a 5.11b 5.11c 5.11d	6c 7a	22 23 24 25	Tiny or missing holds for most moves. Steep to overhanging. Requires problem-solving skills. Ape genes may be helpful.
5.12a 5.12b 5.12c 5.12d	7b 7c	25-26 26-27 27 28	Progressively more difficult problem-solving and movement sequences. Extremely small and limited holds on steep terrain or some good holds on near-horizontal overhangs.
5.13a 5.13b 5.13c 5.13d	8a 8b	28-29 29-30 30-31 31-32	Same as for 5.12 range, but harder. Specific training virtually required. Verges on science fiction, but a fair number of climbers can do it.
5.14a 5.14b 5.14c 5.14d	8c 9a	32 32-33 33-34 34	Unreal! Like climbing overhanging glass. Definitely world-class, but possible.

individual move on a particular route. Thus, a 27-meter 5.9 route could have one move of 5.9 within 30 easier moves of 5.6, or it could involve one 5.9 move after another for the entire 27 meters. Some guidebooks will provide a protection rating by following the YDS rating with an R for *runout*, indicating large distances between intermediate anchor points, or an X indicating nonexistent protection and death potential from falls. Always give yourself some flexibility when exploring a new area for the first time and, when in doubt, select routes conservatively; that is, begin with easier routes and work up the ratings.

Ascent Styles for Rock Climbing

The nature of the rock and the natural features along the route determine the level of difficulty of an ascent, and thus dictate the subjective difficulty rating. Among the different "styles" of climbing a route, however, some add a degree of difficulty without changing the overall numerical rating. Adding difficulty by using a more challenging style can enhance your sense of accomplishment upon completing a route. A series of terms have been standardized to describe the particular style of an ascent of a Class-5 route:

- **on-sight flash**—A complete first-try lead of the route without falls and without any prior viewing or knowledge of the route. The ultimate style.
- **beta flash**—A first-try lead of the route without falls, but after receiving some information, or "beta," about the route or specific moves involved.
- **red point**—A complete lead of the route without falls, following previous attempts or practice on the route.
- **pink point**—The same as Red Point except that the route has been pre-protected with anchor points such that the climber merely has to clip the rope through them.
- **top-rope**—Climbing with the rope already anchored above to virtually eliminate fall distance.

Getting Started

Climbs that involve setting up anchors and using harnesses and ropes can be complicated. This book provides you with the basic fundamentals of moving on rock, selecting and using equipment, and ideas for training to improve your climbing. However, there is no adequate substitute for personal instruction from a qualified climbing instructor or guide. Specific safety techniques are presented throughout the text, but if a technique or concept is misinterpreted and incorrectly practiced, the consequences could be serious or fatal.

Many universities offer beginning rock-climbing instruction, and local climbing organizations and clubs often hold seminars and classes. Information on what is available can usually be found at your local outdoor equipment store. The American Mountain Guides Association (listed in the Appendix) can also help you identify rock-climbing instructors and guides in your area.

Rock climbing is a partner sport. Even bouldering usually requires a partner to spot you for difficult moves. You will need to be selective when identifying a climbing partner, because your life may depend upon this person. Take the time to find someone with whom you can communicate well, and whom you can trust.

An Overview

We will begin by reviewing the array of equipment used in rock climbing. Chapter 2 acquaints you with the gear, from securing yourself into a harness through tying into the rope and clipping into your first anchor. Movement techniques for efficient and enjoyable climbing are presented in Chapter 3. You will also learn more about using technical equipment to enable safe climbing in this chapter. In Chapter 4 you will learn about specific training that can improve your climbing performance. Chapter 5 is a colorful and exciting tour of classic crags around the world. This chapter should conjure up a few dreams and future vacation plans. Many rock climbers also enjoy using their skills on the world's high mountains, where the routes may pass over ice and snow in addition to rock. Basic introductions to ice climbing and Alpine mountaineering are found in Chapter 6. This chapter also contains some tips about competitive rock climbing. At the end of the book you will find an informative Appendix that has an extensive list of resources for additional information and a Glossary of both technical and slang terms used in rock climbing.

GONE TO THE HAPPY HUNTING GROUNDS

It is nestled among the pines in the Hawk's Nest area of Devil's Lake State Park, Wisconsin—24 meters of adventure on slick red and purple quartzite. The new crop of upstart, sport-climber hotshots flash it on-sight; a rather aggravating exhibition, since it took me five years to move through the main crux. Of course, I only attempted the route a half-dozen times over that period, but still . . . . The one consolation is that everyone who goes up it comes down with blood-engorged forearms, sweaty brows, and more than a bit of oxygen debt. At least now I know the route is supposed to be difficult.

Until a year ago, I thought it was the route *R-Ex,* which was rated F9B in the archaic system of the Devil's Lake guidebook. The F9B rating would translate into something around 5.9+ to 5.10a in any other source. Difficult but not impossible for a fortyish, absent-minded professor type. The initial 12 meters were worked out on the first day of attempts, before the crux moves stalled me just below an excellent, or "bomber" (short for bombproof), horizontal edge. I knew that edge was the key. I would be home free up the top 12 meters if I could just get it with a right hand. The next year it happened! I stemmed my foot out right onto a sloping hold, lifted the left foot a few inches higher into the base of the small dihedral, and r-e-a-c-h-e-d . . . yes! The bomber—I had it! I was off to the top! But, wait . . . reality check . . . I was going nowhere. I pulled up on the bomber and locked off the arm with my elbow tightly flexed, but nothing appeared for the left hand and there was less for the feet. So, I just hung there, locked-off with my forearms gorged with blood, or *pumped*, until I fell. And that's the way it went for the next three years: huff up the crack, reach delicately for the right pocket, power into the layback, crank, crank again, stem and reach for the bomber, pull and lock off, hang . . . pump . . . fall.

Not all visits to Devil's Lake were spent locked off on *R-Ex*. After all, other classics such as *Charybdis* (5.8), *Anomie* (5.9), and *Alpha Centauri* (5.10d) are within 9 meters of it—hard routes that I could actually do. *Alpha Centauri* actually began to feel easy. Still, after climbing these great routes, I would glance over at *R-Ex* and shrug.

At some point during those years I realized that I had misinterpreted the Devil's Lake guidebook. What I thought was *R-Ex* was actually the route *Happy Hunting Grounds* and was rated F10a in the guidebook's system. It could possibly be called 5.10d, maybe even 5.11a, anywhere else. This allowed me to rationalize my lack of success and provided an excuse to repeat the other routes instead. I did occasionally try it, however, and even revealed it to other climbers. I watched a few of these lock off on that bomber, reach up with the left hand and levitate over the bulge, meander up and around the blocks, and finally work under the big roof and out to the anchors. Some did it after a try or two—Todd, Miles, his brother Bill, even "Gumby." However, I watched more than these few lock off at the bomber, pause, then fall and lower to the ground huffing and complaining about getting pumped and ruining the rest of the day.

Then, on a recent spring morning, I watched as Paul flashed it! Paul, who has only been climbing a couple of years, huffed and grunted a bit through the lower moves then locked off the "bomber," reached, grabbed, and floated up to the roof. Teenagers!

Then it was my turn. After a two-year sabbatical from *Happy Hunting Grounds*, I was tied into the rope and pulling up the lieback to set up the reach for the bomber. Although the moves were not the smoothest, they went. I got four fingers on the hold, pulled, locked off, pumped . . . and fell.

It's easy to become obsessed with a route, but I know there are about a zillion reasonable routes out there, so an obsession is simply not justified. With this thought I untied from the rope, munched a Pop-Tart, and enjoyed the sun through the pines. A few other friends tried the route and one actually got the bomber, but even this one locked, pumped, and fell. Paul had to leave for home and, a short time later, my family started packing up for the hike down to the parking lot. My rope hung unoccupied on *Happy Hunting Grounds*.

Within a short time I was tied in and headed up again for my usual lock off, pump, and fall. After one go from the usual perspective, I allowed a more exploratory glance out to the right, around the subtle corner, and spied a small triangular pocket big enough for a toe. I switched hands on the bomber to a left cling in order to reach the pocket, then finger-tipped a "little nothing" bump up on the right as I lifted my left foot high into the shallow dihedral. Careful balance then allowed a release of the bomber, a reach higher to a shallow, sloping hold, then a right hand up to a good bucket. I heard trumpet fanfares! Fireworks lit the sky! The rest of the route to the roof was pure joy.This now classic route presented some wild positions as I moved tenuously under the dark ceiling, then delicately out to the right, searching for the reach over the lip and the holds leading up to the anchors. The holds appeared just in time, and I levitated out and up to the top. Whew! I even did the crux moves again just to be certain. Later, the six-hour drive home from Devil's Lake seemed brief as it was filled with pleasant visions of moving up the route. After five years, this adventurous 24 meters to the *Happy Hunting Grounds* had finally become a familiar path.

2

ROCK CLIMBING EQUIPMENT

Your safety and success in rock climbing depend, in various degrees, upon your equipment. A visit to the local climbing shop or a look through one of the current gear catalogues can be a real eye-opener. A wide variety of equipment is available these days, and the price tags may seem excessive, particularly because maintaining a reasonable margin of safety often precludes the purchase of used items.

Fortunately, the natural progression in climbing—from bouldering to top-roping and, eventually, to leading ascents—enables a gradual accumulation of the necessary items. Technical climbing involves two or more persons, and most climbers will pool their equipment at the crag; for instance, one partner supplies the rope and the other the anchor gear.

Bouldering requires minimal equipment: a well-fitted pair of climbing shoes and a chalkbag will usually do. Top-rope climbing requires a rope and anchor gear, but it is still relatively inexpensive in comparison with many other exercise and sport activities. Traditional lead climbing requires a wider assortment of anchor devices and associated gear, but even the expense of a lead-climbing setup can be minimized without compromising safety.

Choosing a Rock Shoe

There is universal agreement that the one item of gear having the most impact on rock-climbing performance is footwear. Rock climbing was originally practice for mountaineering, and early climbers would slip and slide up the rock in stiff, unresponsive mountain or hiking boots. Through trial and error, climbers finally figured out that the softer rubber soles of basketball shoes worked much better, though their extreme flexibility caused problems on steep face climbs. The first shoes designed specifically for rock climbing incorporated smooth rubber soles for high friction, a stiff forefoot for secure stances on small rock edges, and lightweight materials to save weight. The specialized rock-shoe design came into its own in the 1980s with the development of a special rubber for the soles and *rands* (the sides of the shoes). This "sticky" rubber enabled climbers to stand on tiny, rounded crystals as well as wafer-thin edges.

Just over a decade ago, there were perhaps two or three brands of rock shoe from which to choose. Today, there are all-round styles that perform well on all types of rock and terrain as well as exotic specialty shoes designed for very specific types of climbing. A magazine recently reviewed over 40 different rock shoe models that ranged in price from around $90 to over $140. Because virtually all modern rock shoes have sticky rubber soles, the most important considerations when making a choice are fit and the balance between stiffness and flexibility.

Although you can get rock shoes through outdoor equipment mail-order companies, it is best to actually try on various models. Stores that carry rock-climbing gear, and indoor climbing gyms in particular, often rent shoes that you can try out. Watch for "demo" festivals where several companies provide shoes for you to test.

Fitting a Shoe

Wearing rock shoes has been described as the "agony of de feet." Contemporary shoe designs have eliminated pain and foot injury as the price you pay for a shoe that performs well. Still, you want to ensure that your foot will not slip or rotate inside of the shoe and that there are no air pockets, particularly in the forefoot area, that can collapse and bend when you transfer your weight to the foot. Thus, a snug fit remains essential.

Generally, you will wear a size or two smaller than your street shoes. The actual fit for a given size varies considerably among shoe manufacturers, and even among styles offered by the same supplier. Again, it is very important for you to try several sizes and models for the best fit. Some climbers wear a lightweight liner sock, but most wear their shoes over bare feet to ensure a sensitive feel for the rock texture. Whatever your preference, the shoe must fit.

You can expect all rock shoes to stretch a bit. Lined shoes will stretch less and feel tight longer; however, they may offer less sensitivity on subtle rock textures. Unlined shoes will shape to your foot and initially provide comfortable, precise performance, but may stretch several sizes with use. Newer, unlined models use special stitching patterns to lessen stretch without sacrificing flexibility.

Stiffness Versus Flexibility

The right balance of stiffness and flexibility largely depends on the type of rock and terrain over which you will be climbing. A stiffer shoe performs well in continuous cracks and on steep face climbs that require edging the soles on small, sharp features. Once these shoes are set and weighted on small rock edges, the stiff sole provides a virtual ledge to stand on. On the other hand, very stiff shoes offer little advantage on lower angled friction climbs where maximizing the contact area between rubber and rock is important.

When contact area and the ability to "grab" holds is critical, a flexible shoe will provide superior performance. Many of the very difficult modern sport climbs, and indoor climbing walls in particular, require a flexible shoe that allows you to feel and adjust to subtle features in the surface.

A rock shoe should have a fair amount of rubber extending around the toe and along the rands of the shoe. Sticky rubber rands are essential for crack climbing where the shoe will be wedged or "jammed" in the crack during moves.

The climber who wants to enjoy the steep cracks of Yosemite, the smooth friction of Stone Mountain, and the sharp, crystal edges of the Rushmore Needles by using a single pair of rock shoes might consider a moderately stiff all-round model for that initial purchase.

© Phil Watts

Different types of rock shoes (left to right): all-purpose shoe, structured edging shoe, unstructured flexible shoe, lightweight slipper.

All rock shoes will eventually break down in structure or stretch and become sloppy. Once the correct fit is lost, performance will diminish. Proper care and attention to wear on the soles and rands, however, should enable you to use a shoe for two to three years.

Caring for Your Shoes

- Minimize wear on the soft soles by limiting walking and standing in your shoes. If you must keep them on while you are not climbing, wear a large sock over the entire shoe.
- Protect the soles from excessive dirt and any oily residues. An occasional light brushing with a brass suede brush can help restore "stickiness" to the rubber surface.
- Allow shoes to dry out thoroughly between uses to prevent rotting of the stitching.
- Resole your shoes before the rands are damaged. Half-soles can be put on for a small fraction of the cost of shoe replacement, but be sure to have an experienced rock shoe cobbler do the job. Resoling services advertise in all of the mountaineering and rock-climbing specialty magazines.

Chalk

By minimizing the effects of hand and finger sweat, gymnastic chalk (magnesium carbonate) can increase your ability to grip holds. Chalk is typically carried in a hand-sized chalkbag, which is either clipped to the climbing harness or tied around the waist on a cord. You can get a chalkbag for around $12 to $15, and a block of chalk for just over $1 from stores that carry climbing gear.

Although most climbers use chalk, it does present a problem from an ecological standpoint. The natural beauty of many rock crags and formations has been marred by countless white dots left from the chalked hands of climbers. The use of chalk has sometimes been characterized as a form of littering. In most cases chalk will wash off in the next rain; however, on heavily used routes and under overhangs and roofs, it may remain for generations. The impact of chalk may be minimized through conservative use and periodic cleaning of the rock by concerned climbers. Always check with local climbers or recreation area managers concerning an area's unwritten ethic or established rules concerning the use of chalk.

Choosing a Climbing Harness

When I began climbing, I would simply wrap the rope around my waist and secure it with a bowline knot backed up with a couple of overhands. Simple, yes, but to fall meant a painful constriction and near suffocation as the rope rode up over my lower ribs. I soon switched to a "swami-belt," made by wrapping strong, tubular nylon webbing around my waist several times and tightening it with a waterknot. The rope was then tied around the swami-belt and secured with a figure-8 follow-through knot. This was a slight improvement, but my waist still absorbed all of the force of a fall. As a result, I stuck to easier routes to avoid falling, and consequently limited my progress and skill development.

A wide array of commercial climbing harnesses are now available that are comfortable, lightweight, and strong. The Union Internationale des Associations D'Alpinisme (UIAA) has set strength standards for climbing harnesses, and all main-brand commercial harnesses meet or exceed these standards. Harness designs are available that are specifically tailored for men, women, or children. The harness must fit snugly around your waist at the top of the hip bones, and the waist-belt must be long enough for you to double it back through the buckle system. Because various models and styles may have subtle fit differences, try several on before making your final purchase.

HARNESS FEATURES

The price of a harness generally reflects the particular array of features it offers. Prices range from $35 to $80.

1. The harness weight will not usually affect its overall strength much and may seem trivial because all harnesses are relatively lightweight. However, a lighter harness may be critical for success on the most severe sport climbing routes. Generally, the lighter the harness, the greater the cost.
2. For summer climbing in shorts or tights, a standard, nonadjustable harness is the most economical choice. However, adjustable leg loops may be useful if you climb in colder weather with more clothing or share the harness with a friend of different proportions.
3. Ease of use is more than a convenience in stressful situations where complexity can lead to error and potential accidents. A quality harness should operate simply and be easy to wear and remove.
4. The availability of attached gear loops provides an easy way to transport anchor devices and other small equipment.

SAFETY TIP

Proper use of your harness is essential for safety. Harnesses differ in how they are secured on the climber, but most involve a double-pass buckle through which the waistbelt webbing must be doubled back. Check your buckle system (and your partner's!) before you begin a climb and frequently throughout the day. Harnesses also differ in the proper method of tying into the rope, so be sure to get specific instructions concerning your harness. Protect your harness from chemicals that damage nylon and from unnecessary abrasion. Inspect your harness frequently for damage and abraded stitching, and retire it when you have doubts.

Selecting a Rope

The natural progression from bouldering is technical Class-5 climbing with a rope. When you are trying wild moves and pushing your limits, falls are to be expected, so don't skimp on your main line of protection—the rope. Fortunately, modern, dynamic climbing ropes, tested and approved by the UIAA, do not break under normal use. On the other hand, ropes can be cut by falling rock or sliced by being stressed over a sharp edge of rock. Improper use always invites disaster, so learn the correct procedures with your lifeline.

Climbing ropes have evolved from strands of natural manila fibers, which were questionable at holding falls, to today's strong, nylon *kernmantle* (core and sheath) ropes. The usual dimensions of kernmantle ropes are 50 meters (1 meter = 3.28 feet) in length by 10 to 11 millimeters (1 millimeter = 0.39 inches) in diameter. Normally, you should avoid shorter ropes because many established climbing routes assume that the climber is using a rope of at least 50 meters. On lead climbs it can be unnerving to run out of rope before the next anchors. Some ropes are specially designed to be used doubled; they range from 8.5 to 9.0 millimeters in diameter.

The specific qualities of note for modern ropes include the number of test falls held, impact force, static and impact force elongation, weight, and water repellency. Rope manufacturers will include this information on a tag attached to all new ropes. Depending on the rope's specific characteristics, prices normally range from $130 to $180 per 50-meter rope.

Characteristics and Ratings of Climbing Rope

The UIAA tests and rates dynamic ropes for use as a single rope or as double ropes (two ropes used together). The principle UIAA test involves a worst-case scenario fall test to determine the number of 5-meter falls of an 80-kilogram (1 kilogram = 2.205 pounds) weight that a 2.8-meter section of rope can withstand before breaking. Most single ropes will average between 5 and 12 falls in this severe test. A rope must survive a minimum of 5 falls to earn UIAA approval. Impact force, or the expected force on the climber and any anchors, is also measured during the standard fall test and must not exceed 11.8 kiloNewtons (kN), or 2,650 pounds (1 kiloNewton = 224.8 pounds).

The UIAA static-tension test determines the degree or percentage of stretch over a 1-meter section of rope under an 80-kilogram load. Single ropes must not stretch more than 8 percent, and an approved double-rope must not stretch greater than 10 percent. The dynamic stretch built into climbing ropes reduces the impact forces on the climber and anchor system, but also increases the overall distance of a given fall and the chance of hitting something on the way down. Thus, the UIAA standards provide a reasonable compromise.

It should be noted that these UIAA ratings are for dynamic ropes specifically designed for rock climbing. Ropes are available that possess strong static qualities (very little stretch under force), but these can result in severe stress loads on a fallen climber and on the anchor system. Static ropes are usually used for rappelling and as fixed lines for descending into and ascending out of caves. Usually, it is best to avoid static ropes for technical rock-climbing applications.

Rope weights depend on diameter and specific construction designs, averaging between 65 and 80 grams (1 gram = .035 ounces) per meter for 10 to 11 millimeter single ropes. Ropes designed for use in double-rope systems are lighter, at 45 and 55 grams per meter; however, two ropes are required.

You can usually purchase ropes with or without a water-repellent coating. Ropes treated for water-repellency are called *dry* ropes. Such treatment reduces the rope's tendency to soak up water that otherwise would increase the rope's weight and decrease its strength. Some feel that the water-repellent treatment improves the rope's resistance to abrasion as well. If the added cost and weight can be tolerated, most climbers prefer dry ropes.

Retiring a Rope

No one really knows exactly how long a rope should last, and the core of the rope may be damaged without any visible problem in the sheath. In general, most climbers will retire a rope after four years regardless of frequency of use. However, if you use your rope on most weekends, perhaps two years is more acceptable, while extensive use may require more rapid turnover. Exposure to a severe, long fall justifies immediate retirement of the rope. Keep in mind that top-rope falls, as opposed to falls while leading, are much less stressful on the rope because the overall fall distances are usually quite shorter.

Stacking and Coiling the Rope

When you pull the rope from your pack, look around for a good location to place it. Avoid tossing the rope into the dirt or other debris. Special rope bags are available that open out into a ground-cloth on which to lay out the rope, although a jacket or stuff-sack works just as well.

Most climbers will transport and store their rope in a coil. However, when in use, the rope tends to tangle less when randomly stacked. Lay out one end of the rope to the side so that it will be easy to find, then stack the rope in a neat but random pile.

When you want to move to another route you will need to neatly coil the rope. There are several effective methods of coiling, but most climbers use some variation of the *butterfly coil.* To execute this coil, match the two ends of the rope and pull through about three double arm-lengths of rope to leave free. Now begin pulling through double arm-lengths and laying these *butterfly wings* over alternate sides of one open hand. When you get to the doubled end of the rope, split the difference across your hand. Wrap the free ends several times around the coil below your hand then push a bight, or bend, of the remaining rope through the eyelet formed by the wraps. Thread the doubled free ends through this bight to secure the wraps, and the rope is ready for storage.

You can rig the butterfly coil to carry on your back by laying each free end over a shoulder, then wrapping them back across the rope coils and your waist. Secure the free ends in front with a square knot, and you are ready to scramble.

Taking Care of Your Rope

Once you have purchased a new rope, proper use and care is essential to ensure many hours of safe climbing:

- Protect your rope from dirt and other debris as much as possible. Never toss your rope into the dirt at the base of the crag. Use a ground-cloth, pack, or jacket to stack the rope on. Also, avoid stepping on the rope, as this can grind sharp particles of sand and dirt through the sheath and into the core.
- Minimize exposure of your rope to excessive heat and the sun's ultraviolet rays. Consider storing your rope in a stuff-sack or custom rope bag when not in use.
- Avoid exposing the rope to any substance that is harmful to nylon, including certain solvents and corrosive products.
- Do not lend out your rope. Who will treat it with the same care as you do? For the same reason, never purchase a used rope.
- Inspect your rope frequently for visible damage. Remember, though, that the core may be damaged without any visible evidence. When in doubt, retire the rope.

Tying In—The Figure-8 Follow-Through Knot

The standard knot used to connect the rope to your harness, a procedure called *tying in*, is the figure-8 follow-through. This is a solid knot that becomes tighter when force-loaded, yet can be untied reasonably easily when you wish. A figure-8 knot is first put into the rope about three feet from the end. The free end is then threaded through the harness (check your harness design, as the proper way to thread differs among models) and the figure-8 rewoven, or followed-through, until the end exits the knot in a direction away from your harness. You must leave at least three inches of tail to prevent the end accidentally slipping part way through the knot in a fall. Check your tie-in knot often during a climbing outing.

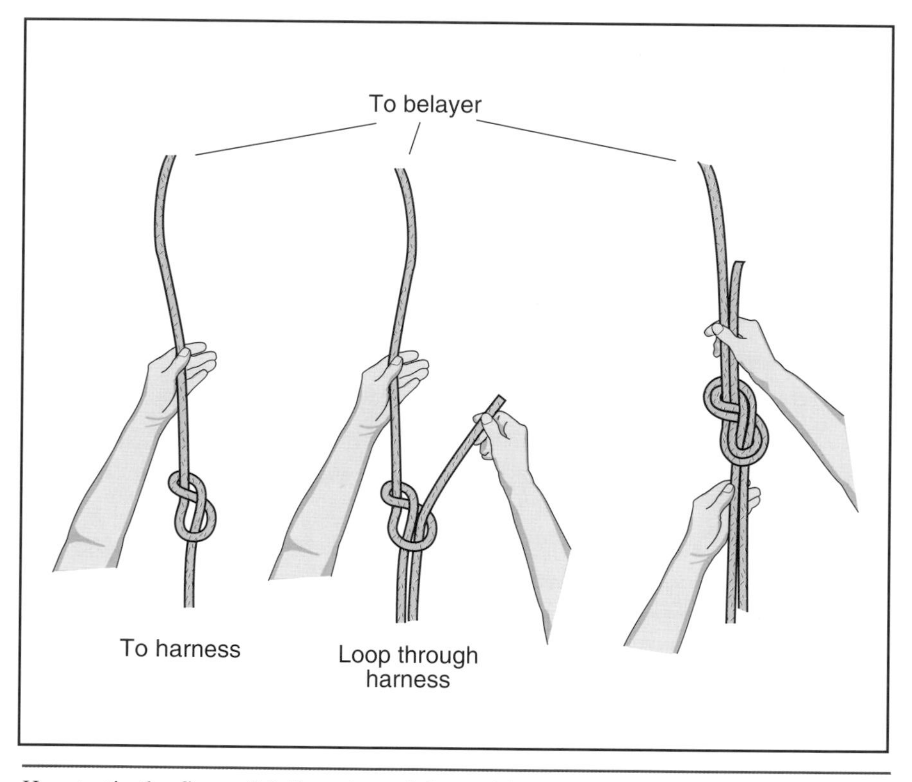

How to tie the figure-8 follow-through knot. Always leave at least a 7.5-centimeter (3-inch) tail when the knot is pulled tight.

Connecting the Anchor System

Technical Class-5 climbing always involves one or more anchor systems that secure the rope and climbers to the rock or ground. Whether the anchors are sturdy natural features such as trees and boulders, or some type of artificial anchor device (discussed later in this chapter), the connection to the climbers and rope must be strong and easily used. Anchors usually are extended by nylon webbing loops (*runners*), and eventually connected to the climber's harness or to the rope using metal snap-links (*carabiners*).

Runners

One-inch tubular nylon webbing is the mainstay for making runners (sometimes called *slings*), although widths of 14.3 millimeters and 17.5 millimeters are available as well. A 1.7-meter length of webbing is normally tied into a loop using a waterknot for a standard-length, or single, runner while 2.9 meters are tied to make a long, or double, runner. In top-rope climbing, where tree and boulder anchors may be several feet back from the cliff edge, longer lengths of 6 to 9 meters are often convenient.

One-inch tubular nylon webbing is both strong—over 1,800 kilograms breaking force—and inexpensive at approximately $1.00 per meter. You can also purchase runners pre-sewn with bar tacks, which provide greater strength and less bulk than knotted runners. Of course, sewn runners are a bit more expensive and do not provide the versatility of changeable length that tied runners do.

A newer and stronger fiber now available for sewn runners is Spectra, which is, pound-for-pound, about 10 times as strong as steel. Spectra runners are available in a 15.8-millimeter width and are always pre-sewn because Spectra does not hold knots well. Spectra is more expensive than tubular nylon and must be protected from heat due to its low (300-degree Fahrenheit) melting point.

Joining Two Ends of Webbing or Cord/Rope

The waterknot is used to join the ends of a strand of webbing to form a loop or runner. Begin with a basic overhand knot, then follow the overhand back through with the other end of webbing. Pull the knot together tightly and leave at least 7.5 centimeters for each tail. Remember, never attempt to tie Spectra with a knot; it will slip easily and come undone under low forces.

The grapevine knot is more appropriate for round material like cord and rope. Once tied, set the knot tightly. As with the waterknot, 7.5-centimeter tails should be left in the free ends.

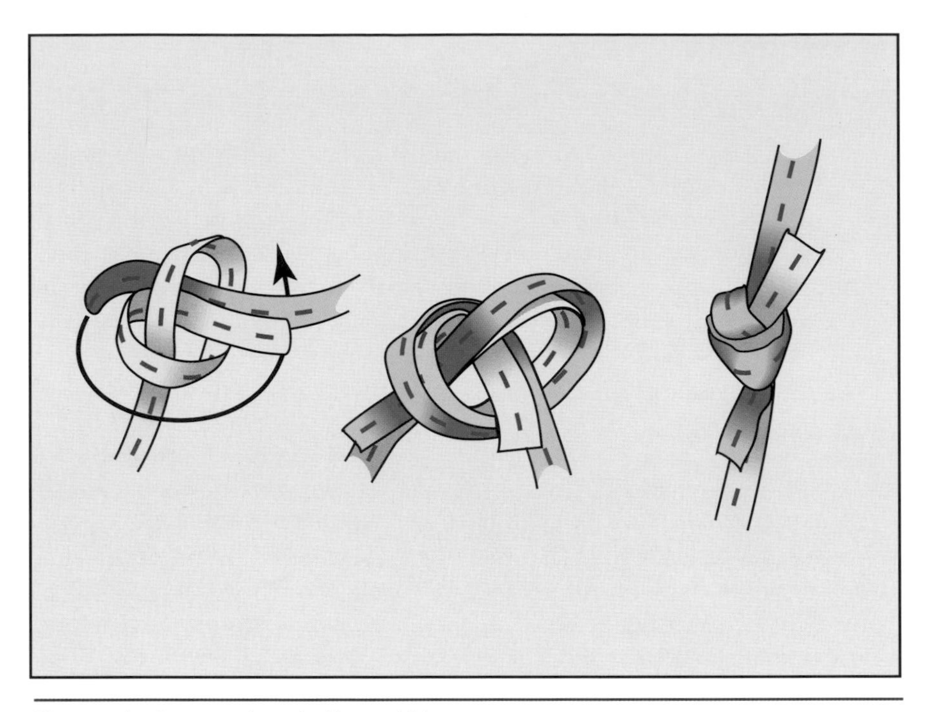

How to tie the waterknot in flat webbing.

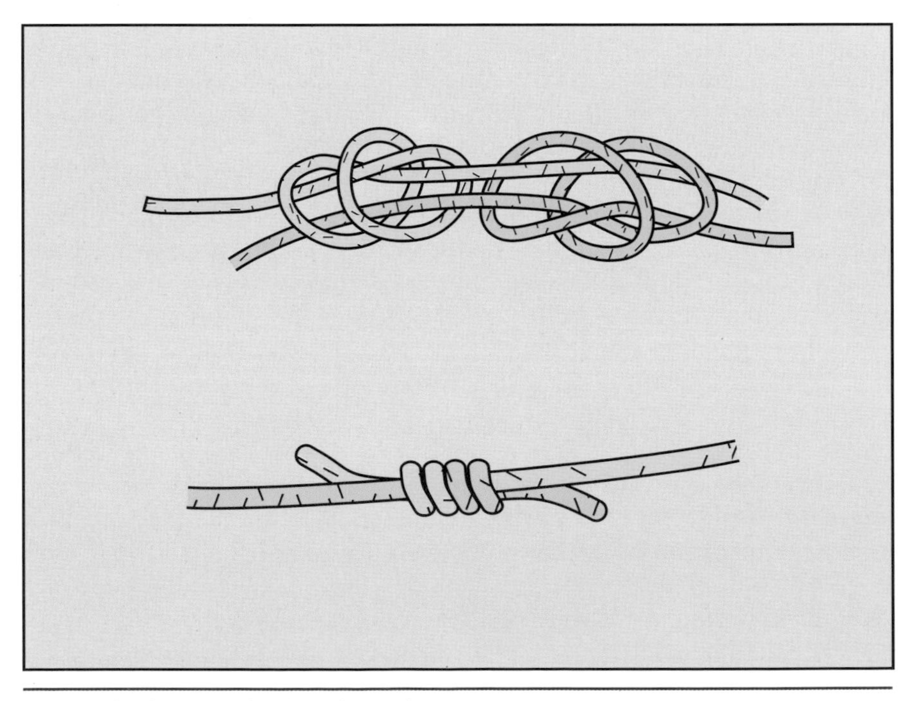

How to tie the grapevine knot in cord or rope.

Carabiners

Before you begin technical rock climbing, you will need to obtain a selection of carabiners. These aluminum alloy snap-links are used to connect the various components of the climbing system. Carabiners are designed with a spring-loaded gate which can be opened to accept the rope, webbing loops, or anchor connections. In order to obtain UIAA approval, a carabiner design must test to a minimum breaking strength of 19.5 kiloNewtons along the spine, or solid side, and 4.0 kiloNewtons along the gated side. Most "biners" will be rated well above these minimum values.

Carabiners are available in three basic designs based on their overall shape. *Ovals* are symmetrical, with the point of maximum length midway between the spine side and the gated side. These biners are very versatile and enable positioning with the gate up or down. *D-shaped* biners are longer along the spine side than the gated side. This results in forces being directed more along the spine side and a stronger design per weight unit than the oval. Thus, a slightly lighter D biner can be several hundred kilograms stronger

Carabiners (clockwise from top): Standard oval, standard-D, asymmetrical-D, bent-gate D, locking D, HMS.

than a standard oval. Asymmetrical, or *offset*-D carabiners, are wider at the gate opening end to enable easier clipping of the rope without sacrificing the strength advantage of the D shape. A modified asymmetrical-D biner, popular for leading sport climbs, is the *bent-gate*-D. The bent shape of the gate on these biners provides a larger gate opening, which makes clipping the rope easier.

Many of the standard-D, and larger asymmetrical-D, carabiners are available with gate-locking sleeves. These *locking biners* provide an increased margin of safety in situations where the gate may be accidentally bumped open. Locking biners are available in screwgate designs, where the gate sleeve must be screwed manually into place, and in twistlock designs, where the sleeve is spring-loaded and snaps into the locked configuration upon release.

One useful modified locking carabiner is the pear-shaped, or HMS, biner. These large, offset-locking D biners accept a large volume of clipped materials and usually are used in a special rope belay technique called the *Munter Hitch*.

AT A GLANCE: CARABINERS

Design	Advantages	Disadvantages	Price*
Standard oval	Versatile all-purpose design. Low cost.	Lower strength-to-weight ratio.	$4.50-$5.50
Standard-D	Good all-round use. Stronger than standard oval.	Less versatile than ovals in some situations.	$5.00-$6.00
Asymmetrical-D	Very lightweight, while retaining strength of the D shape. Easy to clip and unclip.	Normally must be oriented with the gate downward. Can unclip easier than standard oval or D. Expensive.	$7.00-$13.00
Bent-gate-D	Same as asymmetrical-D plus larger gate opening; easier to clip. Mainstay for sport climbing.	Same as asymmetrical-D. Should only be used for the rope-end of connections.	$7.00-$13.00
Locking (various designs)	Lock system prevents accidental opening of gate. Increased strength. Mainstay for belay and top-rope anchors.	Heavy and costly for standard overall use. Special designs are expensive.	$7.00-$20.00

**Prices in U.S. dollars.*

SAFETY TIP

The gate is the weakest link in all carabiners. Avoid set-ups that put pressure sideways across the biner and onto the gate. A carabiner's strength is reduced by more than 50 percent when the gate is open, so make sure your biners snap closed easily and completely when released.

Belay Devices

The set-up and techniques of managing a climber's rope and catching falls is called the belay. I remember my first belay lesson. I was clipped into an anchor at the top of a 12-meter quartz crag with the rope wrapped around my waist for friction and the free end grasped in my gloved hand, ready to

Belay devices (left to right): ATC plate, Sticht Plate, Figure-8 ring, Munter Hitch.

increase the body wrap when the climber fell. And fall he did, all 200 pounds of him. Somehow I hung onto the rope with vice-like fingers as it painfully tightened around my waist and my breathing temporarily stopped. This was the body-belay experience, a good skill to know for emergencies, but I was encouraged to quickly place an order for a mechanical belay device.

Belay devices increase the friction on the rope during a fall, which enables the belayer to control the force generated by the fall. Most belay devices are modifications of the slotted Sticht Plate invented in Germany in the 1970s, through which a bend of rope is passed and the loop clipped into a locking carabiner. The system is then clipped to the front of the belayer's harness. Mechanical belay plates make holding the rope during falls relatively easy and have eliminated the friction burns common with the body belay.

Several belay device designs are available. Modifications of the original Sticht Plate design provide excellent friction yet resist locking up against the rope. Figure-8 belay devices allow for smooth rope management, but many provide less friction than a plate design. Prices average around $13 to $15 for either design.

There are a couple of specialized belay devices available that secure the rope during a fall even if the belayer's brake hand is off the rope. Such auto-locking belay devices assure that a belayer will not "drop" a fallen climber. These are, however, about four times as expensive as a basic belay device, and should not be relied upon as substitutes for a knowledgeable and experienced belayer.

Many belay devices will also work as a friction mechanism for rappelling back to the ground after an ascent. For those long or multiple rappels, it is wise to acquire a figure-8 descender ($11-$15), which will better tolerate the heat buildup from friction.

Artificial Anchors

Anchors are used in a variety of circumstances in rock climbing, and must always be strong and secure. Some of the best anchors are established by tying off natural features such as trees, large blocks of rock, chockstones, or rock horns. When natural features are unavailable, artificial anchor devices are used. Artificial anchors are designed to fit into cracks or pockets in the rock and are available in a variety of models.

A small selection of artificial anchors will suffice for most top-roping situations. However, traditional lead climbing demands additional pieces and a wider range of designs. Sport-style climbing requires only a *quickdraw*—a short runner with two carabiners—to clip into each fixed bolt anchor along the route. Still, it may be wise to purchase a few anchors to back up or supplement the fixed anchors on some sport routes.

Nuts, Hexcentrics, and Tri-Cams

The most basic design for an artificial anchor device is a tapered metal wedge called the *nut* or *chock*. The nut is placed above or behind a constriction in a crack in the rock which, if all goes well, will prevent it from pulling out. Most nuts are tapered in two dimensions, which enables the piece to fit two sizes of crack.

Some older nuts have holes through which a loop of 5 to 8 millimeter perlon (nylon) cord is threaded and tied with a grapevine knot to provide a carabiner clip-in loop. Most modern nuts, however, are swaged on strong steel cables that provide the clip-in loops. Nuts range from approximately 7/4 millimeters to 38/28 millimeters for height/width sizes and withstand dynamic forces from 2.5 to over 10.0 kiloNewtons. Prices for wired nuts range from about $6 to $8 depending on the size.

Hexcentrics are six-sided aluminum alloy chocks that can fit four different crack sizes each. The smallest hexcentrics come wired; however, most are threaded with Kevlar, Spectra, or the newer Gemini cord, which is tied with a grapevine knot to secure a clip-in loop. Unwired hexcentrics are not rated for strength because the type of cord and knot used for the clip-in sling determines the weakest point. Given a strong, well-tied cord, hexcentrics are one of the strongest forms of artificial protection available. Hexcentric prices will range from $6 to $9 each, but the cost of the cord for the clip-in sling must be added.

A hybrid between nuts and hexcentrics is the *Tri-Cam,* made by Lowe Alpine. Tri-Cams look a bit like nuts, and may be wedged as such, yet their unique shape enables them to fit unusual contours in the rock. The big advantage of this design is the rounded shape that tends to rotate and wedge tighter, or *cam*, in a crack when force-loaded. When the clip-in sling is wrapped between the two spine rails and the piece is set with a strong tug, the force of a fall will result in increased pressure of the Tri-Cam against the rock. While learning to place Tri-Cams correctly may take patient practice, they are very strong at 8.4-20.4 kiloNewtons depending on the size. Eleven sizes are available, ranging in price from $13 to $39 each.

Nuts and hexcentrics are relatively lightweight and inexpensive as artificial anchors go. A selection of 8 to 10 nuts and hexcentrics of various sizes will likely suffice for all of your top-rope climbing needs. If you plan to lead up some traditionally protected routes, a larger selection will provide more versatility and the necessary extra pieces for intermediate anchors. If your budget allows, Tri-Cams make a more versatile substitute for hexcentrics.

Spring-Loaded Camming Devices (SLCDs)

The first active camming anchors appeared in the late 1970s and were called *Friends*. These unusual-looking devices involved four kidney-shaped camming units spring-mounted to a single axle and rigid stem. A cable and trigger mechanism allowed one to easily contract the cams for placement in a crack, while release of the trigger would free the spring mechanism to expand the cams against the rock. This would hold the piece in position even in parallel-sided and flaring cracks. A clip-in sling tied through a hole in the stem enabled attachment of the rope via carabiner. The shape of the cams resulted in a widening of the unit and increased friction if a force was applied through the clip-in sling.

These miracle anchors enabled rapid placement and security in cracks where nothing else would work. With this versatility, an ability to fit a wide range of crack sizes, and high strength, it is easy to see why a SLCD is truly the climber's friend!

Today, SLCDs come in several designs. Most manufacturers have replaced the rigid stem with flexible steel cable that can conform to rock edges instead of risking breakage from lateral forces. Some SLCDs have only three cams to provide a narrower profile for small crack features. One model employs a double-axle design that enables the SLCD to fit a wider range of crack sizes and provides security as a passive anchor even with the cams fully extended.

All of this convenience and versatility does not come cheap, however. SLCD prices range from $45 to just under $70 per anchor. A full-width range of about 18-70 millimeters will require four to seven units.

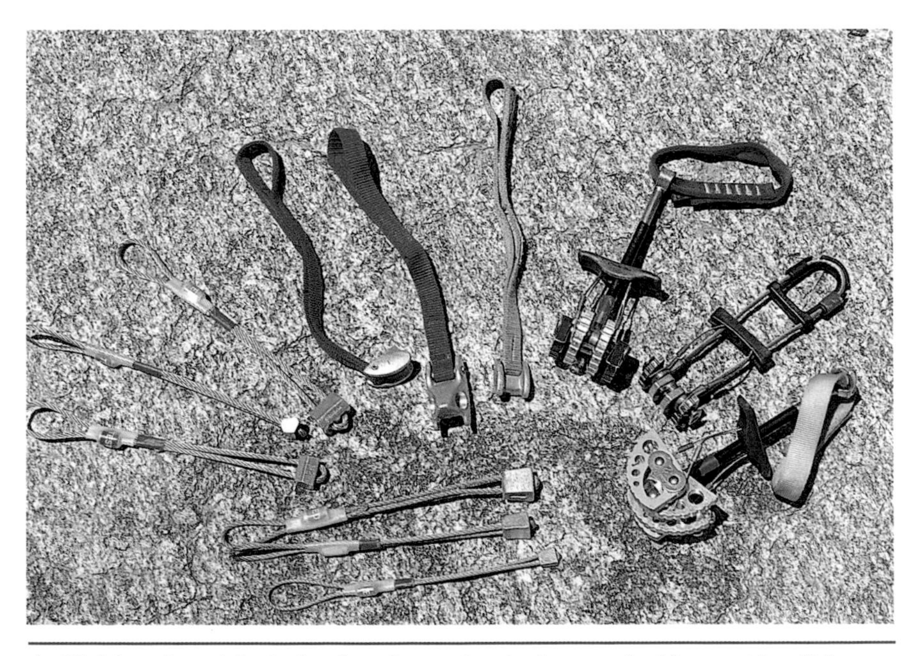

Artificial anchors (clockwise from bottom): wired nuts, wired hexcentrics, Tri-Cams, SLCDs.

Quickdraws

Sport routes are usually protected by permanently fixed anchors. On the more modern routes, the most common fixed anchor is a 9.5-millimeter bolt that is set into a drilled hole in the rock and equipped with a hanger that accepts a carabiner. All you need to attach the rope to these anchors is a selection of quickdraws.

Choose from the many types of quickdraws to attach your rope to the anchor.

A quickdraw consists of a short loop of sewn webbing, usually 14.3-millimeter nylon or 15.8-millimeter Spectra, into which two carabiners are clipped. A standard- or asymmetrical-D biner is used for the clip into the bolt, while a bent-gate asymmetrical-D is convenient for the rope-clip end of the quickdraw. The strength ratings of sewn quickdraw runners vary, but are usually over 20 kiloNewtons.

Prices for quickdraw slings, ranging in length from 127-203 millimeters biner to biner, are $2.50 to $3.50. You will be able to do most bolted sport climbs with 8 to 10 quickdraws; however, longer routes may require 12 or more.

Gear Rack Sling

The collection of carabiners and artificial anchor gear that you will haul around is called the *rack*. You can clip everything into a standard runner looped over your shoulder, but a padded gear rack sling ($12-$15) will be more comfortable.

Some climbers prefer to clip gear to loops that are available on most climbing harnesses; however, space may become limited for the gear necessary for longer, traditional lead climbs. As sport routes require only quickdraws, these harness gear loops are quite adequate.

Protection Maintenance

- Spend some time practicing placement of artificial anchors. This will help you develop an "eye" for the correct size of anchor for a given crack.
- Inspect your protection often to check for damage, especially frays in the wire or cord clip-in slings.
- When the trigger mechanism on a spring-loaded camming device becomes sticky, wash the piece with soap and water, rinse thoroughly, and lubricate the axle with a light spray of Teflon (non-oily) lubricant.
- Retire any artificial anchor that sustains a severe leader fall.

Helmets

If you thumb through one of the current rock-climbing magazines or visit an established climbing area, you will not likely see many climbers wearing helmets. Climbers state many reasons for this lack of head protection:

helmets are too hot; they obstruct vision of the route ahead; they constrain the freedom of climbing; they are not "in style." The fact remains, however, that many serious climbing-related injuries could have been prevented, or their severity lessened, had the person worn a helmet.

A helmet may protect your head from falling rock and other debris, as well as cushion it during tumbling falls. While established crags are usually free of loose rock, the changing nature of the medium urges caution. If you

GEARING UP TO CLIMB

	Gear items	Price*
Bouldering:	Rock shoes	$125.00
	Chalkbag and chalk	$15.00
		Total = $140.00
Top-roping:	Bouldering gear ($140.00) plus . . .	
	Harness	$40.00
	Rope (50 m × 11 mm)	$150.00
	Nylon webbing	
	About 21 meters in assorted lengths	$21.00
	Standard carabiners (6)	$30.00
	Locking carabiners (2)	$15.00
	Belay device	$14.50
	Stoppers/hexcentrics	
	10 in assorted sizes	$75.00
	Nut pick	$6.50
	Helmet	$50.00
	Pack	$40.00
		Total = $582.00
Lead climbing— traditional-style:	All gear listed for top-roping ($582.00) plus . . .	
	Set (4-5) of smaller wired stoppers	$35.00
	Set of spring-loaded camming devices—	
	6 to 8 from 1.5 to 7.5 centimeters	$350.00
	Standard carabiners (25)	$100.00
	Large locking carabiner	$16.00
	Standard nylon runners (8)	$25.00
	Long runner (1)	$8.00
	Quickdraw slings (6)	$20.00
	Gear-rack sling	$18.00
		Total = $1154.00
sport-style:	Shoes, chalkbag, harness, rope, belay device, 2 locking carabiners ($359.50) plus . . .	
	Standard-D carabiners (10-14)	$60.00
	Bent-gate carabiners (10-14)	$90.00
	Quickdraw slings (10-14)	$36.00
	Standard nylon runners (2-3)	$12.00
		Total = $557.50

**Prices in U.S. dollars. All amounts are estimated averages for medium priced items.*

progress to alpine rock climbing and mountaineering, where falling rock and ice are real probabilities, use of a helmet is the norm. I have appreciated my helmet on occasion when, as I concentrated on footwork, I conked my head under an overhang.

When shopping for a helmet, compare only those models that are approved for rock climbing by the UIAA. Make sure the fit is appropriate. Most helmets have adjustable suspension systems to accommodate a variety of head coverings, as weather dictates.

A Final Note on Safe Equipment

Failure of equipment in rock climbing presents a different set of problems than in other recreational activities. Blowing a tire while cycling is an inconvenience and costs time to repair. Fashioning a replacement for a broken canoe paddle in midstream can place a strain on your creativity. In rock climbing, however, most equipment failures will have immediate consequences that are more than inconveniences. Your chances of recovering from a pulled anchor, broken carabiner, or cut rope are minimal to none. When your life is on the line, equipment simply must not fail. These are the three most basic safety points regarding climbing equipment:

- Select quality gear approved for rock climbing by the UIAA.
- Learn how to use each item—practice *before* your life depends on it.
- Take care of your climbing gear. Retire anything that you have doubts about.

3

ROCK CLIMBING CORRECTLY

Movement over rock combines the physical components of balance, flexibility, strength, and endurance with the task of sequential problem solving. Practice and mastery of a few basic climbing principles will enable you to explore the rock and develop your personal style and repertoire of moves.

Rock climbing also demands poise and discipline. There is nothing quite like being high on a windy crag, moving smoothly from problem to problem, working the rock and the protection. Time on the rock will yield a degree of comfort and sensitivity that will enable climbing to become much like a creative dance for you.

This chapter first reviews the fundamental climbing techniques used for various types of rock features. Later in the chapter, the technical aspects of roped climbing are introduced. The techniques involved in moving over rock are best practiced and developed through bouldering, where the intricacies of equipment and inhibitions are reduced. So grab your rock shoes and a spotter, and try out some moves on the boulders!

THE FOUR MOVEMENT PRINCIPLES

Maintain three points of contact with the rock whenever possible. This will maximize your balance and stability, like a tripod steadies a camera. On easier climbs this will be a simple matter of moving one foot or hand at a time. However, on difficult routes, some handholds or footholds may be absent, and you will be forced to get by with less than three-point contact.

Balance over your feet. Since the legs are normally stronger than the arms, you should position as much weight as possible over your feet. This will minimize the forces on your arms. Look around constantly for footholds, and concentrate on positioning your body to maximize your weight over your feet.

Learn to sense your weight transfer from contact point to contact point during movements. Beginner climbers often speak of "fighting gravity"—a limiting misconception. Learn to *use* gravity. It is the source of friction that keeps you on the rock. As you move, your weight is transferred from hold to hold. As you learn to feel this, you will be able to anticipate how gravity will pull you onto or into the next hold. Thus, you can position your hand or foot accordingly. This anticipation will enable you to plan a series of precise, efficient movements through the route's crux.

Learn to rest without coming down. Fatigue causes climbers to become "pumped," and many falls result. Learning to rest on the rock will help you resist fatigue and enable you to climb longer. When holding a static position on the rock, see how much you can relax your grip without coming off. Try different body positions and combinations of holds to find the best rest every few moves. Avoid pulling on holds during rests. Instead, hang from a straight arm while you lower and shake out the other. Keep breathing. Climbing should be as aerobic as you can make it.

SAFETY TIP

Although you will not usually go very high during bouldering, you do hit the ground when you come off the rock. Attention to a few points can make bouldering safer.

- Clear away loose rock and debris from the landing area below the rock.
- Use an alert spotter to help control falls and protect your head and shoulders.
- If the route takes you out of your spotter's reach, set up a top-rope and use it.

Face Climbing

Rock faces come in all textures and angles and demand the greatest variety in hand and foot positions. The keys to success on all but the most overhanging faces are balance and weight transfer. Footwork and body position are critical.

Using Your Feet

Footwork is the most important aspect of face climbing. The two basic methods of standing on face holds are smearing and edging. The rock will dictate which technique is best for a given situation.

Smearing is most commonly employed on lower-angled, slabby rock that lacks definite edges or knobs. The sole of the shoe at the base of the toes is "smeared" onto an indentation, rounded bump, or other irregularity. This maximizes the surface contact area between the shoe rubber and the rock. Weight transfer over the placed foot increases friction and holding force.

Smearing is also useful for tiny micro-edges on steeper rock, as the sole of the shoe conforms to the edge contours. Place your shoe just above the edge, then allow it to slide down and over the hold.

Practice smearing on a variety of rock textures and angles. Look for subtle indentations and features on which to test various foot positions and balance points. Remember, smearing works best when most of your weight is positioned over the foot.

On steep faces, you will need to look for defined holds on which to "edge" the shoe. Edging is most often done with the inside of the foot at the base of the big toe. The strength of this area of your foot and the inherent stiffness of modern rock shoes in this part of the sole provide surprising security on sharp holds. Some climbing problems may dictate that you edge with the outside of the foot, just back of the small toe, or even with the point of the toe—a technique called "toeing-in." Toeing-in is important when climbing pocketed sandstone and limestone, where the lip of the pocket is used as an edge.

Face Climbing

On lower angled slopes, commonly called slabs, you should stand fairly vertical relative to the pull of gravity. This will position your hips away from the rock and your weight directly over your feet. Your upper body may lean forward a bit to allow hand contact with the rock, but the tendency to "hug" the rock should be resisted. Leaning too far in will pitch your weight forward of your feet and lead to slips.

As the terrain becomes steeper, you will need to bring the hips and upper body closer to the rock and the balance point over your feet will become finer. It is important to keep the hands near the level of your shoulders or head during steep face climbing, as an extremely high reach will pull you into the rock too much.

Occasionally on vertical terrain you can lean away from the face using good, bomber handholds to create counterpressure between your feet and the rock. This is particularly useful when footholds are sparse. Make certain that your handholds are solid, and, because this technique is very strenuous, move quickly to a more balanced stance.

Sustained overhanging rock will prevent you from positioning much of your weight over your feet. You must still work to maintain foot contact, however, to reduce the overall load on the arms and provide a base for counterpressure. When not moving, hang on straight arms to place most of the force on your skeleton instead of the muscles. This helps reduce fatigue.

© Phil Watts

© Mary Messenger

Foot techniques for face climbing: smearing (top), edging (bottom left), toeing-in (bottom right).

As with smearing, positioning your body correctly and placing your weight over your feet are critical for effective edging. Both smearing and edging rely on the friction created when you transfer your weight over the foot. Practice both techniques on a variety of terrain to discover how small a rock feature you can stand on without slipping.

On steep and overhanging rock, a foot occasionally will be used like an extra hand to get a partial grip on a hold. One such technique, called heel-hooking, involves kicking up or out to a hold, hooking it with the heel of the shoe, and pulling with the leg until a handhold can be reached.

Radically steep overhangs will often require you to "paw" a hold with the foot, just to keep it on the rock and the weight of the leg off the arms. Since the rock is too steep for you to place your weight over the foot, you must rely on leg strength and counterpressure to maintain the necessary friction.

Regardless of the terrain, learn to place your feet precisely on holds. Once a foot is set, avoid moving it about on the hold until you go into the next move. If your leg begins to shake while holding a foot position, a phenomenon known to climbers as "sewing-machine leg," lower your heel to relax the leg muscles. Precise and efficient footwork will take some practice to develop, but that is the purpose of bouldering.

Using Your Hands

While it may seem that a viselike grip is essential in climbing, in most situations the fingers are simply configured to the hold contours and the body is positioned to enable gravity to pull the hand onto the rock. The larger muscles of the upper arms and shoulders, combined with the lifting action of the legs, are then used to pull the body through the move.

The undercling grip (palms up) is more secure as you move your feet higher.

Types of Grips

Open Grip

In the open grip, the hand conforms to the hold contours; friction from the finger pads supplies purchase. Some holds have positive in-cut edges that the fingers bend around like a hook. The open grip is the least injury-producing hold because the finger tendons are usually spared severe stress.

Cling Grip ("crimper")

The cling grip is used on flat-topped edges or sharp micro-edges. Only the fingertips contact the rock, and the first knuckle is hyperextended to resist collapse of the finger under pressure. When possible, the thumb should be wrapped across the hyperextended knuckles as a brace. Although this grip is very strong, when used on small holds for extreme moves ("crimping") it makes the fingers vulnerable to tendon injury. The fingertips can also be lacerated, or given "flappers," by sharp rock edges.

Wrap Grip

Rounded and knob-like holds can often be wrapped by the fingers or the entire hand. This is one of the most secure grips due to the large contact surface area and greater muscle use. When possible, wraps are done with the outer edge (the "pinkie" side) of the hand against the rock. This usually allows a more balanced body position.

Pinch Grip

When there is no hold edge that gravity can pull your hand into, you will need to use muscle as the source of holding force and pinch the hold. Pinch grips are most useful on small knobs and pebble-like holds. The strongest pinch is often between the thumb and side of the index finger.

There are innumerable precise hand and finger configurations, and it would be superfluous to describe all the options in this text. Exploring the rock to discover what works best is part of the climbing experience. There are, however, four basic hand patterns, or "grips": the open grip, the cling (or "crimper"), the wrap, and the pinch grip.

Two additional hand and arm techniques that are very useful are the undercling and the mantle. The undercling uses an upside-down hold, such as a flake or overhang edge, by gripping with the palm upward. Pulling up and out on the hold, usually by leaning the body out from the rock, provides counterpressure for the feet. The security of an undercling gets better as you move your feet higher; however, the stress on the arms increases as well.

The mantle is used to gain a ledge or flat-topped feature and, as the name implies, is much like climbing onto a fireplace mantle or countertop. With both hands on the ledge, bring your feet up to high holds. Now, hoist your body until one hand can be positioned heel-down to press the body further upward. When your body is up as far as possible above your hands, lift a foot to the ledge. Look for a handhold higher on the face, and stand up on the

Combining a mantle with the arm and a high step to gain a ledge.

ledge. Mantling is a very strenuous maneuver, and, when no good handhold above the ledge is available, standing up may seem like balancing on a flagpole. Whenever possible, it is best to avoid full-out mantles.

Crack Climbing

While cracks make it easy to find a route—you simply follow the line—they often lack horizontal edges to stand upon or to grasp with your hands. The four movement principles still apply when climbing cracks, but purchase for holds must come from a variety of "jamming" techniques for hands and feet.

If you have spent most of your time honing face-climbing skills, exposure to a steep crack can seem foreign and particularly strenuous until the proper techniques become familiar. I experienced this acutely on a route named *Soler* at Devil's Tower National Monument. My partner and I had spent the previous four days climbing knobby face routes in the Needles of South Dakota, but now we hung from two rusty bolts and a solid SLCD in a crack, 46 meters above the ledge where the roped climbing had begun. The rock above was steep and featureless, except for a single, narrow crack that sliced the next 30 meters in a straight line. The moves up this fissure would require pure crack-climbing skills. The various finger pinch and cling grips that we had used in the Needles would not apply here, so we dusted the backs of our hands with chalk and prepared to jam!

In the best crack-climbing circumstances, a finger, hand, fist, toe, or foot is slotted just above a constriction in the crack and pulled or pushed down to wedge against the constriction. In parallel sided cracks—those without convenient constrictions—some type of torque, camming action, or other expansion must occur to jam the appendage in the crack.

Crack types are described according to the predominant hand technique that the crack size dictates. Of course, climbers have different sized hands, which does become a factor, but for the most part the terminology applies. The four primary types, in ascending size order, are finger cracks, hand cracks, fist cracks, and off-width cracks. Larger cracks into which most or all of your body will fit are called chimneys.

Finger Cracks

Finger cracks make for exciting technical climbing. The classic "finger lock" jam involves placing the fingers in the crack, usually thumb down, and locking the knuckles above a constriction. When the arm pulls down, the torque on the hand cams the fingers tightly into the hold. Although the thumb-down position is usually preferable, thin cracks may only admit the fingertips of the pinkie and ring fingers, in which case a thumb-up hand position is required. Whatever the situation, try to get as many fingers as deeply into the jam as possible.

The footwork for finger cracks involves toe jamming. This is where rock shoes with narrow, pointed toes really perform. The foot is turned sideways with the big toe up and the knee out, while the toe of the shoe is placed in the crack. The jam is set by rotating the knee upward and weighting the foot to cam the shoe in the crack. Search out the crack carefully for good toe-jam spots, as finger cracks will not offer much in the way of space for the feet.

You can "leapfrog" your hands up the crack while maintaining the thumbs-down orientation or you can shuffle jams without crossing the hands over. Often it is best to jam one foot in the crack while the other works on face holds to the side of the crack. Practice will enable you to work with the personality of the rock and find the most efficient moves and positions.

Working a finger crack with one foot smearing on the face.

When the crack leans to one side, the hand on that side will usually lead in the thumb-down position. Your body will stay on the downside of the crack, and the foot on that side will probably stay on the face to either smear or edge while the opposite foot jams the crack.

Hand and Fist Cracks

Hand-sized cracks can make for rapid upward progress as secure hand and foot jams are set over and over in rhythmic succession. The classic hand jam is similar to "shaking hands" with the crack. The hand is inserted, thumb up with fingers straight, then the thumb is brought tightly across the palm toward the base of the pinkie. It is this thumb action that expands the hand against the sides of the crack to set the jam. When executed properly in an appropriately sized crack, the hand jam is about as secure as climbing holds get.

© Phil Watts

Classic hand and foot jamming in a vertical crack.

Different crack widths require modifications of the basic hand-jam technique. The fingers may be flexed at the second or third knuckle to provide an arch or tent-like configuration in wider cracks. For jams above the head, the hand may be inserted thumb down and torqued into a secure jam.

As with finger jams, hand jams may be leapfrogged or shuffled. In general, a thumb-down hand jam will be secure when placed over your head, but it loses purchase as you move up and past. The thumb-up jam is most secure at face level and below.

Foot jams are secured in the same manner as toe jams. Turn the foot on its side with the knee outward, slot the shoe in the crack, rotate the knee upward, and stand up on the leg. As with hand jams, foot jams may be leapfrogged, one over the other, or shuffled. Do not set foot jams too deeply in the crack or leg movement will be compromised. A position that accepts the toe and ball of the foot usually provides maximum security.

When the crack is too large for secure hand jamming, the hand may be rotated 45 degrees to enable a fist jam. The fist is placed into position fairly relaxed, then flexed to apply pressure against the sides of the crack. Fist jams may be placed straight in, as if punching the crack, or reversed, with the palm facing out of the crack. The thumb is positioned either outside the fist over the fingers or tucked into the palm. Since there is less ability to expand the hand in a fist position than in the hand-jam position, it is important to recognize slight constrictions and pinches in the crack contours above which to place the fist.

Off-Width Cracks

Climbing off-width cracks—those too wide for fist jams but too narrow to chimney—is awkward, strenuous work. Furthermore, the proper technique seems difficult to master. Such fissures are often referred to as "awful-width."

Fortunately, few modern climbing routes involve off-width technique since contemporary climbers tend to avoid cracks that require it. Historically, however, routes followed natural lines, cracks, and chimney systems, and the most difficult of these involved off-width. You may therefore find short or long stretches of off-width terrain on some of the older "classic" routes.

Off-width cracks are climbed sideways, with one foot and arm inside the crack and the other foot and arm on the outside. Before you launch up an off-width, you need to decide which direction to face as it is usually impossible to switch while in the crack.

The inside arm is usually in an arm-bar position—extended into the crack with the palm pressed forward against the rock and the elbow and upper arm pressed back against the opposite side of the crack. The inside leg struggles to find some combination of counterpressure between foot and knee or knee and hip.

The outside leg must provide the force to move the body upward using a heel-toe jam or working off edges along the outer lip. The outside hand can be used high or low, pushing appropriately to help keep you in the crack.

Occasionally, the crack may narrow down to where the hands can be stacked for a secure jam until the legs are moved up. Of course, you will need to get some type of good hold or jam for the legs, or your hands will be stuck.

Learning crack climbing can be a painful experience as you struggle to develop efficient jamming techniques. Many climbers tape the backs of their hands with cloth athletic tape to protect from abrasions. To do so, first lay a few strips of tape across the back of the hand to form the initial pad. Hold the hand in a slightly cupped position, flexed a bit forward at the wrist. Beginning on the pinkie side of the hand, bring a strip from the wrist area diagonally across the back of the hand, around the index finger, and back to the wrist. Repeat this from the thumb side of the wrist, across the hand, and around the pinkie finger and back. Finally, wrap a couple of complete turns around the wrist to lock the ends of the diagonal wraps. Avoid making the wraps too tightly: Circulation can be impeded and mobility of the wrist and hand limited by the tape.

Climbing Chimneys

When the crack is big enough to accommodate your entire body, it is called a chimney. Chimney techniques vary according to the size of the gap, but ascending always involves some type of cross-body pressure against the sides of the chimney.

Narrow chimneys are usually climbed using pressure between the knees and back. The flexed knees are pressed against the forward wall, while the feet and back are pressed against the back wall. Maximize foot friction by keeping the toes pointed downward and the soles flat against the rock. The hands press forward to stabilize the upper back as the body is ratcheted upward.

In wider chimneys, cross-body pressure is accomplished between the feet and back. Extended legs press the feet against the forward wall, and the arms remain downward with the hands pressed against the back wall. A move is made by pressing down and back with the arms enough to release the back pressure, as the torso slides slightly upward. One foot may kick back against the rear wall to aid in pushing the torso upward. For the next upward move, this foot is extended to the forward wall and the opposite foot kicked back.

Climb narrow chimneys using pressure between the knees and the back.

Counterpressure Techniques

The cross-body pressure used in chimney techniques is a form of counterpressure where force applied in one direction creates another force in the opposite direction. Counterpressure techniques can be used when the forces you must apply to holds are not directly in line with gravity. "Stemming" with the legs to create counterpressure between two lateral holds will often yield a secure, even restful, position. Classic stemming is the technique of choice for bridging the space between the walls of an inside corner.

© Greg Epperson

Stemming to provide counterpressure for the feet.

Face holds may also be stemmed to provide a stance while handholds are searched out. Coming out of a stem on face holds usually requires you to rock your body weight up into a balanced position over one foot. This move is called a *rock-up* and is followed by a step to the next hold by the opposite foot.

Some chimneys are so wide that you must stem completely across the gap with the left hand and foot on one wall and the right hand and foot on the other. The counterpressure produced by this spread-eagle position keeps you on the rock while your hands and feet shuffle upward in small, careful increments.

Stemming techniques are not limited to support positions. Occasionally, your position on the rock, particularly on overhanging faces, will produce a tendency for your body to rotate or swing to one side. This so-called "barndoor" effect can be prevented by stemming a foot out to the side to block the swing. You can also use a counterbalance technique to correct the barndoor effect by "flagging" one leg off the rock, across your midline, and behind your supporting leg.

Flagging a leg to offset the barndoor effect.

Offset cracks and cracks in corners are often "liebacked" using counterpressure by pulling with the arms while pressing with the feet in the opposite direction. Liebacking requires that you maintain good hand contact with the rock since it is the lean off your arms that provides the counterpressure for the feet. Hands and feet may be leapfrogged or shuffled as you move upward. Liebacking is another strenuous technique, but you can minimize fatigue by maintaining straight arms, thus placing much of the force on the skeleton.

© Phil Watts

Pure lieback technique up a corner crack.

Tips for Climbing Overhangs

1. Although you may be unable to position your weight directly over your feet on overhanging rock, footwork is still important. Look for edges, places to hook a heel, and other features that can be used to take the weight of your legs off your arms.
2. Often you can work your feet up high between moves, where they can help push you into position for the next reach.
3. When reaching for a hold, you may need to pull in quickly with the opposite arm and hand close to the shoulder to lock off as you make the next reach. This is a strenuous maneuver, so take aim on the next hold and move quickly. From some positions you can reduce overall arm stress by keeping the support arm straight, instead of pulling into a lock off, and pushing the body upward with the legs.

4. Look and feel for opportunities to use counterpressure, flagging, and controlled but dynamic lunges to avoid strenuous pull-ups. Placing the outside edge of one foot on a hold and twisting the body into the rock on that side may sometimes enable you to reach a high hold with the inside arm—a technique called "twist-locking."
5. Hang on straight arms while in static positions to let your skeleton, instead of your muscles, take most of your weight.

Using a "twist-lock" to reach a high hold on overhanging rock.

Protecting Yourself While Climbing—How to Set Up Anchors

If movement over the rock is thought of as the "art" of rock climbing, protecting yourself with a harness, rope, and anchors is the "science," although a good deal of creativity is involved here as well. Learning the proper techniques for roped climbing is a serious matter since most accidents involve mental errors made by climbers. The use of the figure-8 follow-through knot to tie the rope into the climbing harness was covered in Chapter 2. This chapter concentrates on the anchor system and its integration with the rope to protect the climber.

Of primary importance in roped climbing is establishing solid, fail-safe anchors. In lead climbing, the primary anchor is for the belayer, the person who manages the rope and protects the climber during falls. Most top-rope set-ups will involve two anchor systems, one for the belayer and one for the rope.

Using Natural Anchors

The best anchors are often natural objects and features, such as trees, boulders, and rock horns. One advantage of natural anchors is that they are often multidirectional or able to take forces from several directions. When anchors must be directional and counter forces in one direction only, you must carefully predict the most likely direction that force will be applied in the system. Before using a natural anchor, check to make certain it is solid by vigorously tugging and pushing on it. Some climbers use the "six-by-six" rule for trees: six feet tall by six inches thick at the base; however, this is rather arbitrary. Of more concern is whether the tree is living and firmly rooted.

Natural anchors are connected to the rope or climber using sewn or tied webbing runners and carabiners. The runner is doubled or girth-hitched around the anchor. In the case of tied runners, the webbing loop may be tied directly around the anchor with a waterknot to allow easier adjustment to the correct length. Place the runner close to the anchor's base to minimize torque effects which could break or uproot the anchor.

Using Artificial Anchors

Whether you are setting artificial anchors for a top-rope system or working to get intermediate pro halfway up a steep face route, the principles of using protection gear, called "chockcraft" by some, are the same. You should take time to learn the correct methods for placing artificial anchor devices and practice until you are familiar and efficient with the gear. Setting up top-rope anchor systems with artificial gear enables you to learn the basics in a more relaxed setting than you'll encounter when strung out on a lead with your forearms pumping.

Chockcraft Basics

- An artificial anchor is only as good as the rock it contacts. Inspect the placement site and avoid suspicious, crumbly textures, loose flakes or blocks, and dirty, vegetated slots.
- Select the size and shape that best fits the contours of the placement spot in the rock.
- Use the largest size that will fit appropriately.
- Place the piece such that contact area with the rock is maximized.
- Orient the sling or cable in the direction of the anticipated force.

Placing Nuts, Hexcentrics, and Tri-Cams

As artificial anchors go, nuts are hard to beat due to their simple design and overall strength. The standard nut is tapered on two sides and will fit two sizes of crack. It is always best to place a nut lengthwise to provide maximum contact area.

Some nuts are curved slightly and have "left" and "right" orientations for you to choose between as the crack contours dictate. Find the best orientation to maximize contact with the rock, and, in the case of a parallel-sided crack, assure a wedge with three good points of contact.

Whenever possible, place a nut where the crack not only pinches off in the direction of the most likely force, but also pinches in the outward direction; this helps to keep the piece in the crack. A gentle tug helps "set" the nut in position.

It is important to extend the clip end of wired nuts with a quickdraw or runner to provide a flexible link to the rope. A direct sideways pull on the stiff cable can torque the nut and lift it out of the crack. It is a scary sight for the leader to look below and see her last nut sliding down the rope toward the belayer.

Hexcentrics are a bit more difficult to place correctly than nuts, but, once set, are strong anchors. Hexes offer two placement orientations in the primary lateral position and a third when placed endwise in a crack. The principles involved in good nut placement apply for hexes as well. The uneven sides of a hex and the orientation of the cord can provide some passive camming force when the piece is force-loaded. This camming action is obtained from both primary placement positions, but not from the endwise position.

Tri-Cams

The unusual shape of the Tri-Cam enables it to fit some spots inaccessible to other gear. There are three modes of placement for Tri-Cams: wedged above a constriction like a nut; with the sling threaded between the spine rails

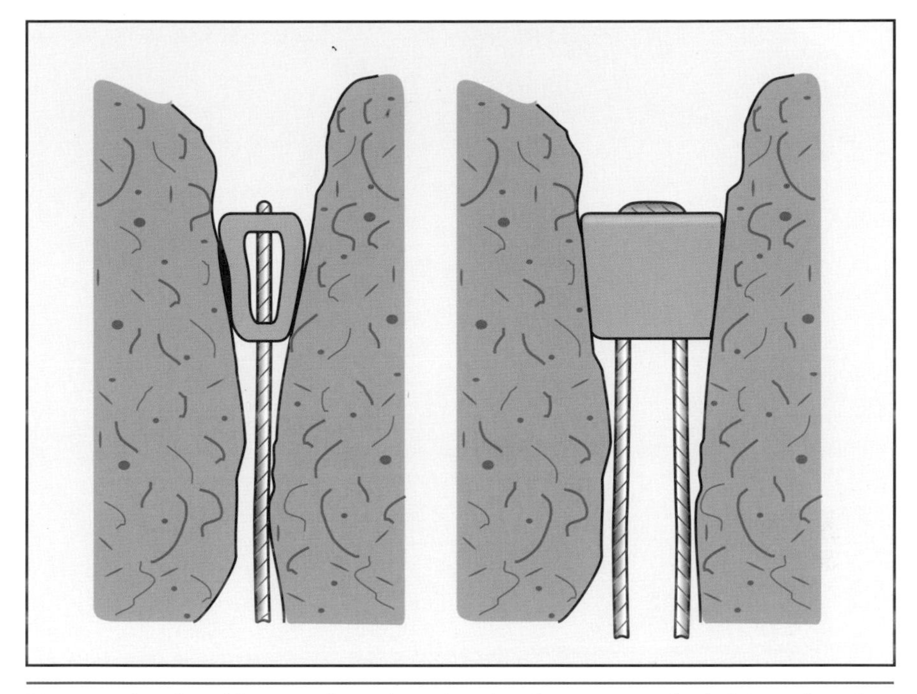

Nuts may be placed in two orientations, but the placement on the left is preferred.

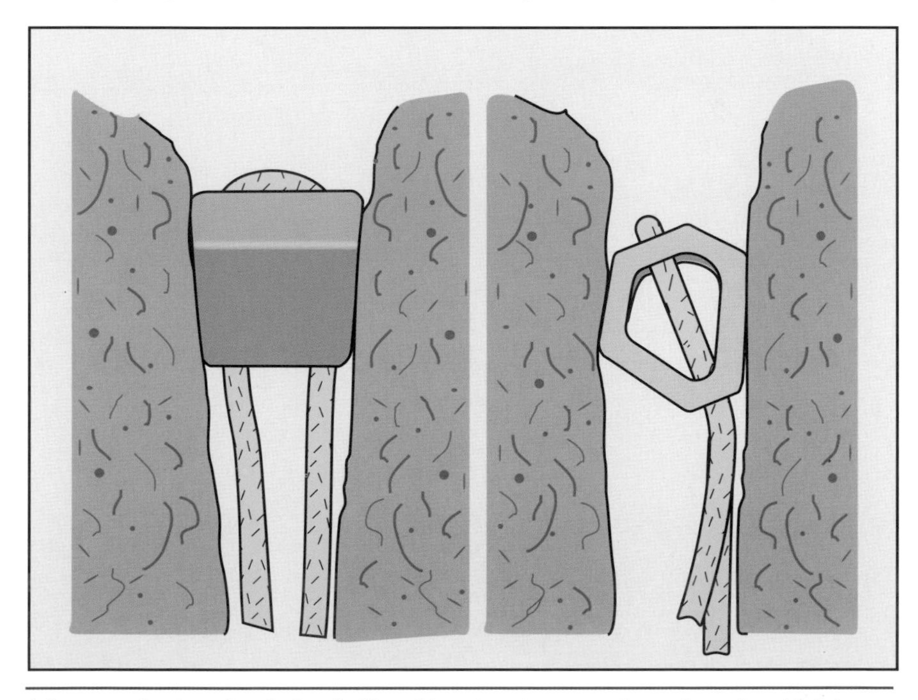

A hexcentric placed endwise (left) and in a passive camming orientation (right).

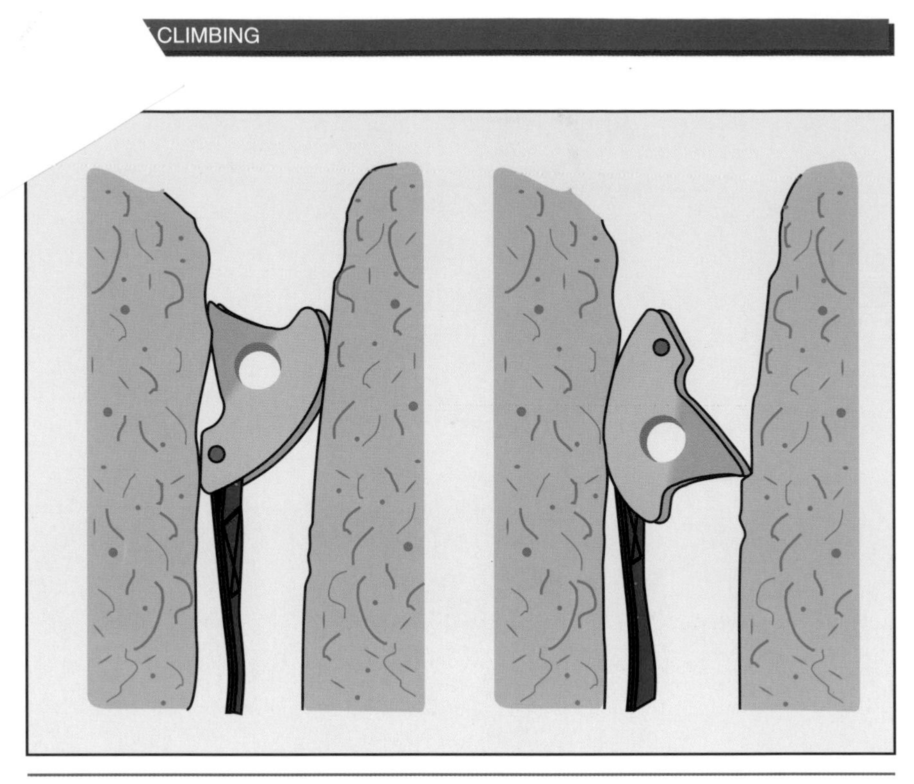

A Tri-Cam placed as a wedge (left) and as a passive cam (right).

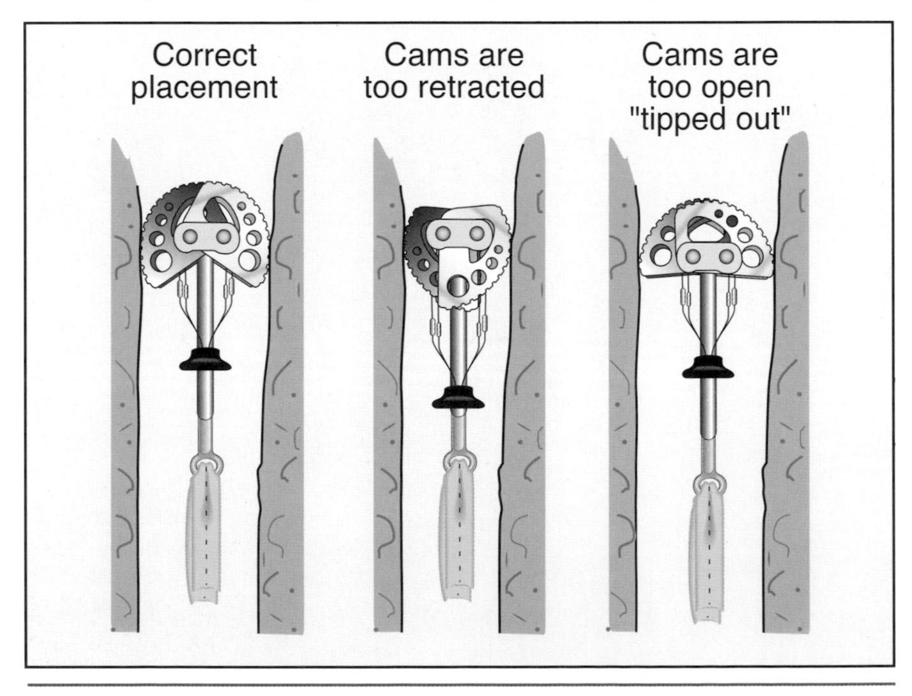

SLCDs are strongest when the cams are evenly set at 10- to 50-percent full deployment.

for passive camming action; and poked into solution pockets, then cammed behind the lip.

When configured as a passive cam, the fulcrum point should be placed in an indentation or behind a bump, with the spine rails against the other side of the crack. All three points must be in contact with the rock, and the piece must be set with a tug. Beware of unstable Tri-Cam placement, and consider extending the sling with a quickdraw, as a sideways pull can rattle the piece loose.

Using Spring-Loaded Camming Devices (SLCDs)

Spring-loaded camming devices are designed to fit parallel-sided cracks that offer no constriction for wedging a nut or hexcentric. The spring-loaded cams provide friction that holds the SLCD in place, while their shape results in a tighter wedge when the unit is force-loaded. Although SLCDs are often touted as "simple to use" and "fail-safe," there are several important points to understand about them.

Most reported "failures" of SLCDs are the result of the units skidding out of the crack. In soft sandstone, SLCDs have been known to skid several inches when severely loaded. Always consider the quality of the rock in which you are placing a SLCD. If the rock is soft or loose, be wary.

If the action of the rope causes the SLCD to wiggle back and forth, it can "walk" deeper into a crack, making retrieval impossible. You reduce this tendency by extending the placement with a quickdraw or runner.

The independent spring-loaded cams on a SLCD enable the unit to conform to irregular crack contours, but the unit may not be as strong when the cams are offset in this manner. The strongest SLCD placements are those where the cams are evenly set at 10-50 percent deployment and the stem or cable is aligned with the most likely direction of anticipated force. A cam is too small for the crack, and its strength and stability will be low, if it is nearly fully deployed, or "tipped-out." On the other hand, if you force a unit with nearly fully contracted cams into a crack, it is likely to get permanently stuck.

Setting Up a Top-Rope Anchor System

The general rule for anchoring the rope for top-roped climbing is to connect a minimum of three independent anchors at the top of the crag. Runners are used to extend the anchor points over the edge of the cliff to prevent the rope from abrading over sharp rock. The middle of the rope is connected to these runners by a minimum of two carabiners, and the rope ends hang to the ground. In this set-up the belayer manages the rope from ground level.

After hiking up a trail or scrambling over easy terrain to the top of the crag, determine the best location for the anchor biners to extend over the edge. Normally the anchor biners are placed at the end of the route. When the route follows a fairly straight vertical line, the rope will always be directly above the climber and falls will be relatively inconsequential. If the route traverses to the side, and the rope line is at an angle, the climber will be exposed to a potentially dangerous swing if she falls. This is called a "bell ringer" and should be considered when locating the upper anchors.

© Phil Watts

A three-anchor top-rope system involving (left to right) a tree tied-off with webbing, a long runner girth-hitched to a tree, and a SLCD in a crack.

Look around for convenient, bombproof natural anchors and placement possibilities for artificial anchors. Once you have established the anchor points, use webbing runners to extend the anchors over the cliff edge. If a single runner must be used to connect two separate anchors, use a self-equalizing slider by putting a twist on one end of the doubled runner before clipping the biners. Avoid directing the runners over any sharp edges that could cut or damage the webbing. If sharp edges are unavoidable, you can pad the runner with clothing or a pack.

Clip a minimum of two carabiners through all anchor runners to accept the rope. At least one of these carabiners must be a locking type. Whenever possible, use two locking biners at the rope connection.

When the carabiners are placed into position over the edge, the extension runners from the anchors must come together at the rope connection such that all angles between runners are less than 120 degrees. Limit the angles to 90

Using a single runner as a self-equalizing slider to connect two anchor points.

degrees whenever possible. Keeping these angles small ensures that no single anchor will have to absorb the total force generated in a fall.

Once the middle of the rope is clipped in and all locking biners securely locked, place the system over the edge such that the gate of the locking biner faces out, away from the rock, with the gate opening positioned downward. The second carabiner should be placed with its gate in opposition to the primary locking biner.

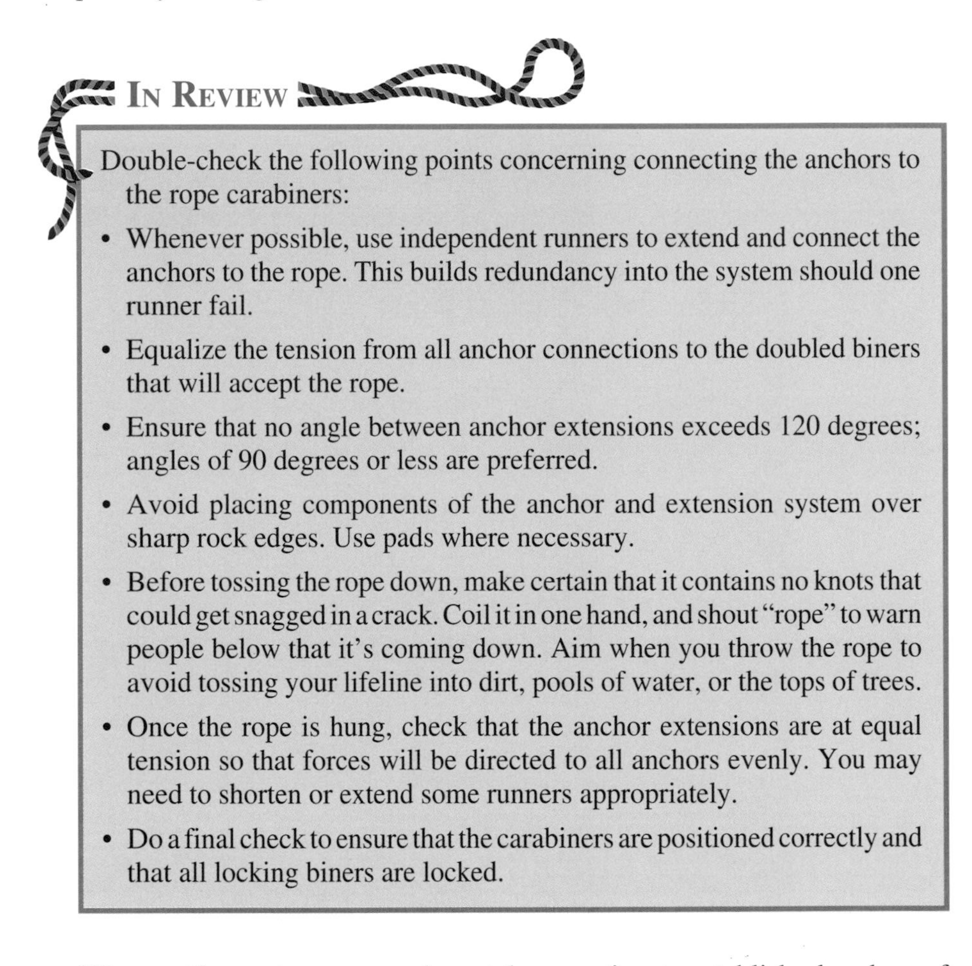

In Review

Double-check the following points concerning connecting the anchors to the rope carabiners:

- Whenever possible, use independent runners to extend and connect the anchors to the rope. This builds redundancy into the system should one runner fail.
- Equalize the tension from all anchor connections to the doubled biners that will accept the rope.
- Ensure that no angle between anchor extensions exceeds 120 degrees; angles of 90 degrees or less are preferred.
- Avoid placing components of the anchor and extension system over sharp rock edges. Use pads where necessary.
- Before tossing the rope down, make certain that it contains no knots that could get snagged in a crack. Coil it in one hand, and shout "rope" to warn people below that it's coming down. Aim when you throw the rope to avoid tossing your lifeline into dirt, pools of water, or the tops of trees.
- Once the rope is hung, check that the anchor extensions are at equal tension so that forces will be directed to all anchors evenly. You may need to shorten or extend some runners appropriately.
- Do a final check to ensure that the carabiners are positioned correctly and that all locking biners are locked.

When setting up top-rope anchors, take your time to establish a bombproof system. If you must work close to the edge while rigging the system, put on a harness and tie in to an anchor. Double-check all knots and connections before hiking down to enjoy the route.

Top-roped routes can be belayed from the top of the rock by arranging the length of the anchor extensions to place the belayer at the cliff edge, facing outward. The anchor carabiners are clipped into the belayer's harness waistbelt and locked. The anchor extensions should be on tension when the belayer is in position lest a fall jerk him over the edge.

While this system provides the belayer with an exciting perch and enables him to top-rope long routes, it does have a few disadvantages. The rope will usually pass over the edge of the rock and could be damaged by a fall or when lowering a climber. Often the belayer will be unable to see the climber, so communication may be difficult. Also, more care is required when exchanging places between climber and belayer at the top of the crag than when on the ground. When the climbing route is short enough to allow the rope to be doubled, the ground belay is the standard of choice today.

Belaying

To belay means to make safe or secure. In rock climbing, the belayer manages the rope and protects the climber if a fall occurs. The belay system consists of three components: the belayer, the rope, and the anchors. The integrity of these components must be maintained, since failure of any one component will usually lead to disaster.

In top-rope climbing, the securely anchored belayer connects the rope through a belay device attached to his climbing harness with a locking carabiner. The belayer then takes in rope as the climber ascends or feeds it out if the climber moves down. Once the route is completed, or the climber wishes to descend for a rest, the belayer slowly feeds out rope lowering the climber to the ground. If a fall occurs, it is the belayer's responsibility to effectively arrest it.

Setting Up the Belay

Take time to decide on the best location and position from which to belay. It may take some time for the climber to complete the route, and once "on belay" the belayer is locked into the system with little opportunity to move about. Place the belay a bit to the side of the climbing route. This will minimize exposure to falling rocks or other debris that could be dislodged by the climber or the rope. Take care not to block access to trails that often follow the lower cliff contours.

Establish an anchor for the belay by girth-hitching or tying off a bombproof natural feature, or use two or three artificial anchors and equalize the tension between these and the belayer. Adjust the length of the runners so that you will be in line with the anticipated fall force and in a stable position tight to the anchor.

Clip into the anchor system via a locked carabiner attached to your harness waistbelt in the back. Due to the friction inherent in top-rope belay systems and the relatively low fall forces generated, the impact on the belayer is not usually great. Many experienced climbers can hold falls easily, and you may see climbers using unanchored belays when top-roping. Still, if the fall comes unexpectedly, the belayer is not well braced, or the climber is heavy, an unanchored belay can quickly become trouble. The belayer can be yanked into the rock face or jerked into the air, causing the climber to fall a greater distance. Solid, natural anchors are almost always available at the base of top-rope routes—use them!

Managing the Rope

Once you are securely anchored, determine which hand is in the best position to provide the brake for the belay. Rig the rope appropriately through your belay device to place the free end in this "brake" hand. The other hand, or "guide" hand, will grasp the rope leading to the climber to assist in paying out or taking in rope as needed. Put a large knot in the free end of the rope, or tie into your harness, to prevent the rope from slipping completely through the belay device.

When belaying a climber, it is imperative that the brake hand never leave the rope. As the climber ascends, you take in rope with the guide hand as the brake hand pulls the slack through your belay device. To reset the brake hand, slide your guide hand back up the rope and reach a couple fingers across to grasp the brake end of the rope ahead of the brake hand. Without releasing the brake hand, slide it down the rope to your belay device. Release the guide hand from the brake end of the rope, and you are set to take in another cycle of slack.

If a fall occurs, or the climber needs to be supported by the rope, apply a brake by bending the rope across the belay device with the brake hand. You can lower the climber to the ground by gradually releasing the brake position to a point where the rope can slowly slide through the brake hand. The speed of descent is controlled by the amount of bend in the rope across the belay device and the tension of your brake-hand grip. Leaning back on the rope will help you maintain balance when lowering the climber.

Keep your attention focused on your climber. He is depending on your alert and effective belay. The more popular crags are often crowded, as are indoor climbing gyms. When a lot of action is going on it may be tempting to watch and talk with others. Such distractions are dangerous—a moment's delay in braking could allow several feet of rope to slide through your belay device before you can react.

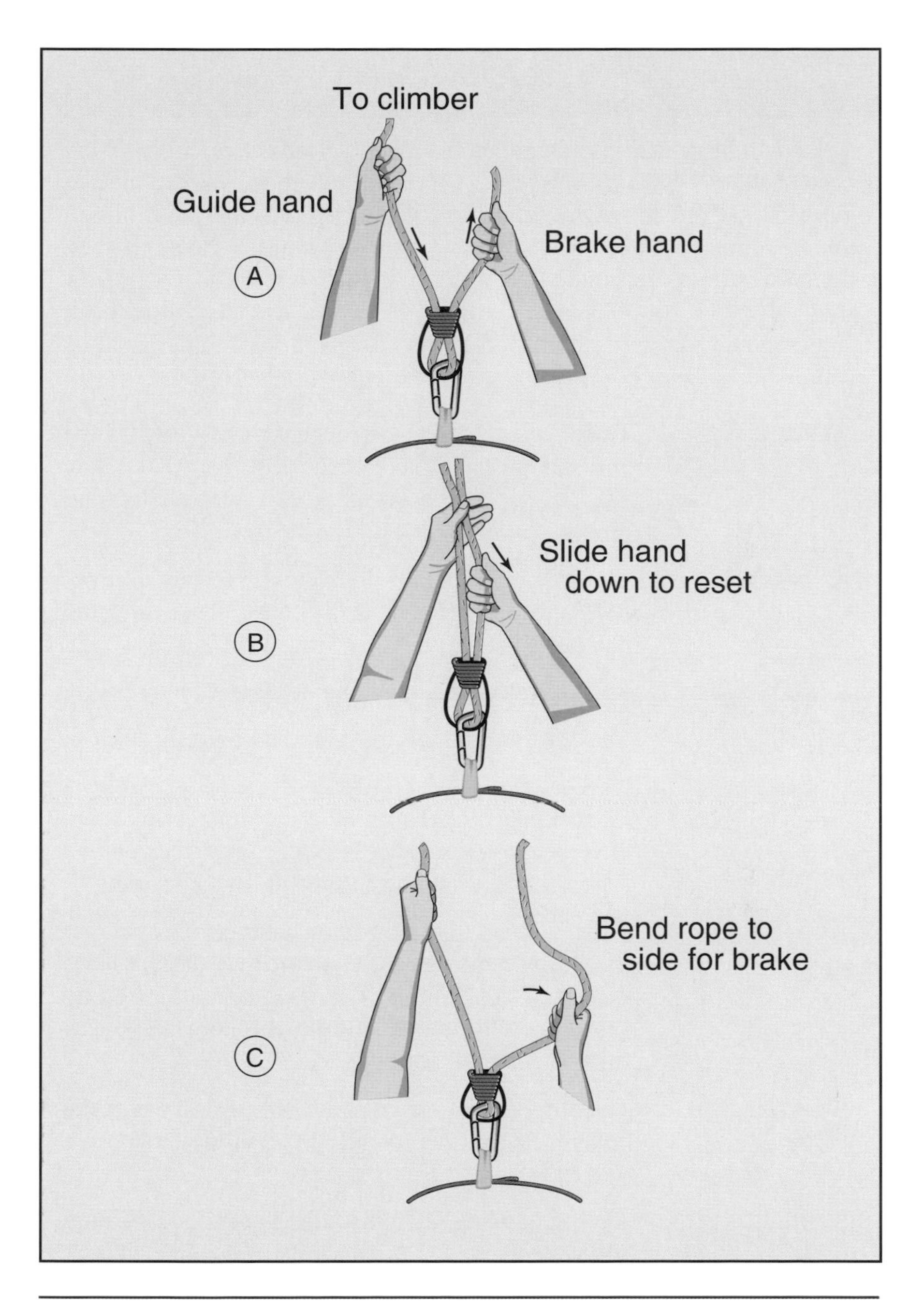

A. Pull in slack through the belay device with the brake hand. The guide hand may assist. **B.** To reset, slide the guide hand up the rope and grasp both strands above the brake hand. Without releasing the brake hand, slide it back down to the belay device. **C.** Apply a brake by bending the rope across the belay device with the brake hand.

HOW TO COMMUNICATE

There will be occasions when the belayer and climber are not in visual contact and must use verbal signals for communication. Many crags are close to loudly rushing water and, high on long lead climbs, the wind can muffle normal conversation. Even as a way of double-checking each other's readiness to begin, it is a good habit to use a standard set of shouted verbal commands at all times. In crowded areas follow each command with your partner's name to avoid mistaking another group's command for your own. A list of standard commands follows.

"On Belay"	The belayer is ready to accept responsibility for the climber. She has double-checked her harness buckle, anchors, tie-ins, belay device set-up, all locking biners, and brake hand.
"Climbing"	The climber is ready to ascend. He has double-checked his harness buckle, tie-in knot, and the belayer's set-up.
"Climb"	The belayer signals the climber that he may begin.
"Up rope"	The climber asks the belayer to take in any slack in the rope.
"Slack"	The climber signals that he is moving down or that the rope is too tight. The belayer should feed out the rope about half a meter for each "slack" signal.
"Take"	The climber wants to hang on the rope. The belayer should apply a brake and expect to hold the climber's weight until he signals that he is moving again by shouting "Climbing." (Some climbers use "Tension" instead of "Take.")
"Watch me!"	The climber is worried about falling and wants the belayer to be very attentive and ready to apply a brake.
"Falling!"	A climber who is actually falling may have the time and the presence of mind to shout this. The belayer should apply a secure brake and brace for the catch.
"Rock!"	A loose rock, or other debris, is falling. Watch out!

"Off belay"	The climber is secure at the top, anchored, on the ground, or otherwise does not require a belay.
"Belay off"	The belayer is taking the climber off belay. The command should be used before the belay is actually dismantled.
"Got me?"	Used by the climber at the end of a top-rope or sport route to assure that the belayer has a brake on before releasing his hold to be lowered.
"Lower me"	Used by the climber when he wishes to be lowered back to the ground.
"Thank you"	A generic acknowledgment by either the climber or the belayer that the last command was heard.

SAFETY TIPS

The most common top-roping accidents result from mental errors committed by climbers. Keep these four tips in mind to protect against them:

- Make sure everyone has confidence in the anchors and the belay system. Are all knots tight and all locking biners locked? If there is any doubt, keep working to make the system fail-safe before climbing.
- Make certain your harness buckle is doubled-back and your tie-in knot is complete and secure. Check your partner's as well.
- Pay close attention when you are belaying. You must respond quickly and effectively to the climber.
- When you finish the route, make eye contact with your belayer, shout "Got me?", and get a definite confirmation that she has a brake securely on before you begin to descend.

How to Begin Leading

While proper use of equipment and technique may eliminate much of the risk in top-rope climbing, lead climbing is a different game. Fall distances, and the consequent forces generated, can be severe for the leader, who is high above his last protection. Furthermore, most falls place force directly on single protection pieces instead of the bombproof, three-anchor top-rope system. When leading out the rope, you must know what you are doing and be able to do it under pressure.

This section will summarize the basics of lead climbing, but is no substitute for hands-on instruction by an expert. Before you begin leading, spend a lot of time working with artificial anchors on the ground. Setting up top-rope anchors is a good way to practice. Serve as an "apprentice" partner for an experienced and safe leader. The role of "seconding" the climb will give you experiences working with gear under pressure, yet with the rope above.

The guidebook to a particular crag or area is a good resource for selecting those first leads. Pick out a clean route that has a lot of cracks for protection and is rated well below your current climbing ability. Work with a competent partner to set up a strong, anchored belay at ground level. Organize your gear, double-check everything, and you are ready to go!

HOW TO "RACK" THE GEAR FOR A LEAD

The gear carried on a lead climb is usually organized, or "racked," on a gear sling worn over the head and shoulder. As you will want to be able to find a particular piece quickly, it is a good idea to use an organized and consistent pattern.

Rack artificial anchor devices, one per carabiner, with the gates up and inward (toward your body). The larger pieces should be toward the back; the smaller wired nuts, several per biner, near the front. Clip four to eight free carabiners in chains of two or more at the front to use with wired nuts or when extending pieces.

Put the rack on first, then place several standard runners, with one carabiner each, over your head and opposite shoulder. A few quickdraws should be made up and carried on your harness gear loops or the gear sling.

When to Place Protection

A good part of the lead-climbing experience is reading the rock for protection opportunities. Many variables come into play, and the protection will differ from climb to climb. In general, protect the route as well as you can—your life may depend on it. There are several principles to keep in mind:

- Protect early and often in the lead. Very little rope plays out in the first stages of a route, which means less stretch length and higher impact forces in a fall. Also, you are "bouldering" without a belay until you get in that first piece of protection.
- As you proceed up the route, maintain as straight a line of rope as possible. You can use quickdraws or runners to extend placements that are out to the side of the main line.
- Extend all wired nuts with a quickdraw or runner, as rope movement can torque such pieces out of the crack.
- Avoid long "runouts" without protection. Fall distances will be at least twice the distance between you and your last protection piece, and rope stretch will add to this distance. Be especially wary of groundfall potential due to large distances between pieces.
- Protect whenever you can and definitely before the crux moves. Any good stance or rest position is a good place to get in some pro.
- Work for solid anchor placements. This is where practice proves invaluable.

Using Runners to Keep the Rope Straight

When stopping a fall, the highest anchor piece usually takes the force in a downward direction. The rope, however, pulls tight to form a straight line between the climber and belayer. Any pieces lower in the system will be stressed in the line of pull of the rope. If the rope zigzags up the route, the pull can be directed outward and upward and the pieces yanked out. This is called "zippering" the protection.

This problem is minimized by using quickdraws or standard runners to extend any anchor placements that are to the side of the direct line. This also helps reduce the "rope drag" or friction of the rope against the protection biners as the climber moves upward. Of course, such extensions will increase your fall distance, so avoid extremes; better to adapt to the route or accept the increased rope drag.

Orient the carabiner that will accept the rope with its gate downward, facing out and away from the rock. This makes it easier to clip in the rope.

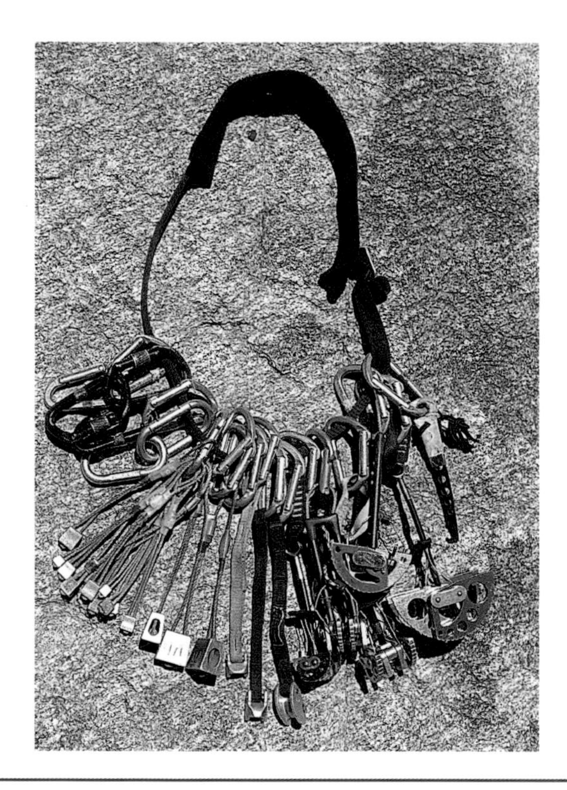

A typical "rack" for traditional leading.

SAFETY TIP

When you clip the rope into protection, consider which side of the placement the route will follow and clip so that your end of the rope exits the biner on that side. If you clip to one side, then move across to the other side, the rope can unclip from the biner as it catches a fall.

Consider Your Second

Consider your partner, or "second," who will be coming up next and retrieving the anchors as she climbs. While protection is always placed in the best interest of the leader, avoid making it difficult for your second to reach an anchor.

When traversing a route sideways, the second risks a severe swing if she falls. As leader, you will want good pro before the crux moves; however, your second will appreciate pro *after* the crux. You should place protection at regular intervals during traverses and routes angled to the side to protect the second.

Anchoring at the End of a Lead

The key to setting up a good belay at the end of a lead is selecting the best available spot and working creatively to structure a bombproof anchor system. Look for a ledge or stance with available anchor points, preferably some natural features and bomber cracks for gear. Keep track of how much rope you have left as you climb so as to avoid coming up short in the middle of nowhere. The belayer should call out how much rope is left at predetermined intervals measured in meters or feet. Set up the anchor system so you can belay directly in line with the run of the rope. Establish a minimum of three solid anchors that are directed for a downward pull and one or two anchors directed for an upward pull. Connect and equalize the anchor points into a central clip-in point and secure this to your harness with a strong locking biner.

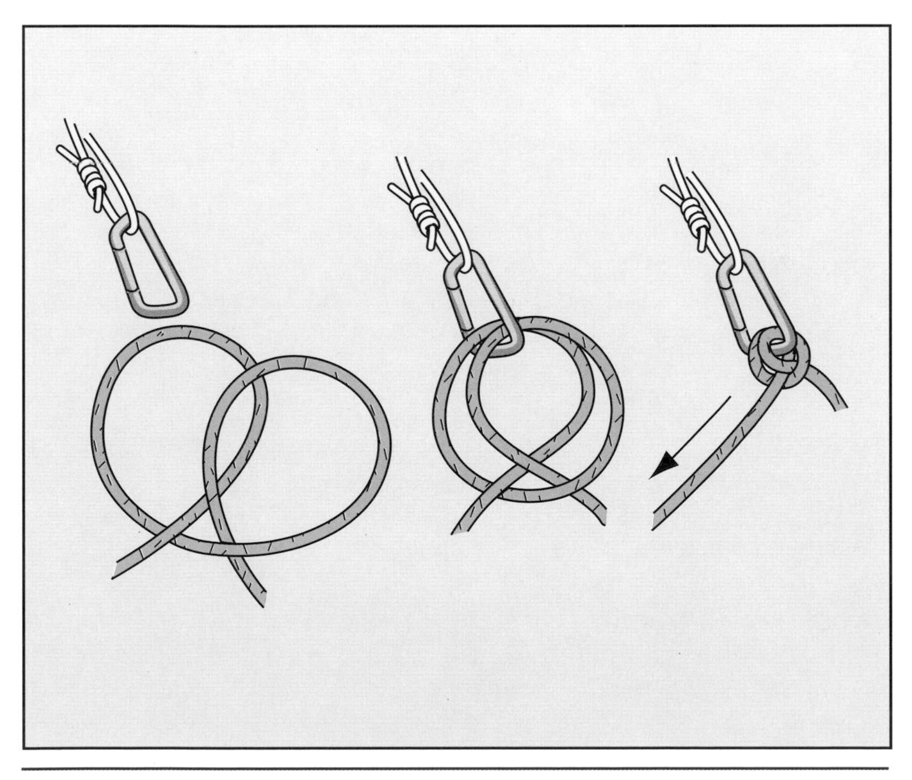

How to connect the rope to an anchor point using the clove-hitch knot.

You can use the climbing rope to connect the anchors by tying the adjustable clove-hitch knot onto the carabiners extending from each anchor point. This method is fast, and the clove hitch is easy to adjust, but take care that any load placed on the system will be equalized to the anchors.

If you have enough extra runners, use them to extend the anchors to a master tie-in point with a big locking biner. Two anchors can be extended by a single, long runner using the self-equalizing slider system described earlier in this chapter. Make certain that you clip the anchor biner through a twist-loop on one end of the runner.

A popular system for connecting the anchors employs a 4.9-meter length of 6 to 7 millimeter static perlon cord that is tied into a loop, or "cordelette," using the grapevine knot. The cordelette is clipped into all anchor points and a loop is pulled down tight from between each anchor then tied, along with the main loop, into a clip-in point via a figure-8 knot. Your master tie-in biner is then clipped into this end loop.

There are countless variations for setting up anchors, so understand the principles and be creative when necessary. Practice on the ground first.

When possible, belay at the edge, facing out, to prevent the rope from

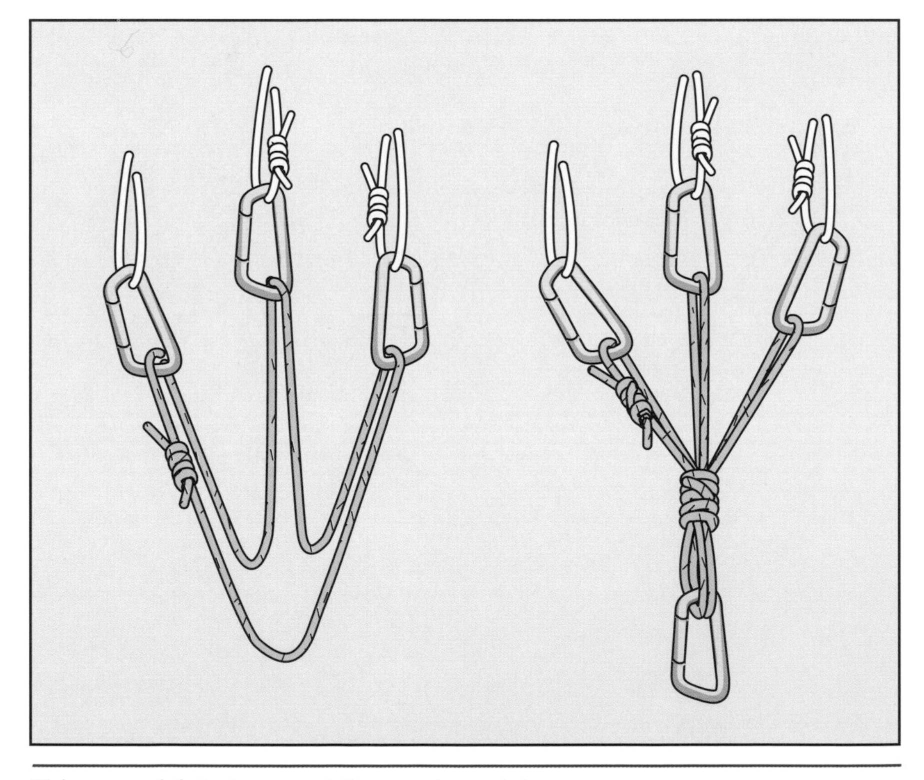

Using a cordelette to connect three anchor points.

abrading over sharp rock. Make sure you are tied off tight to the anchors to avoid getting pulled over the lip by a falling partner.

Once you have set up the anchors and are securely connected to the system, you can call out "Off belay!" While your second prepares to follow the pitch, you should gather any excess rope and stack it neatly on a nearby ledge. If there is no convenient ledge, you may need to drape the rope across your lap or over a leg. Keep the stack neat to avoid tangles. When you have all of the slack taken up, place the rope through your belay device, double-check everything, then call out to your partner, "On belay."

How to Belay a Leader

Belaying a leader is not necessarily complicated, but it does differ from the straightforward top-rope belay. As with all belays, it is imperative that you be attentive and remain focused on the climber. Listen closely for verbal signals as well.

You will pay out the rope as the climber ascends. Don't allow slack to develop, but be careful of pulling directly on the climber or magnifying rope drag. Feed out the rope quickly as the leader clips protection, then take in the slack after the clip is made. Rope is then taken in as the leader moves up to and past the protection, at which point you begin feeding it out again.

Seconding a Leader

The second plays several roles during an ascent. Initially the second will be the belayer for the leader. Once the leader is off belay, the second can begin dismantling the belay anchor system. Maintain your connection to at least one solid anchor, however, until the leader has put you on belay.

You should carry a runner, slung over the head and shoulder, on which to clip the protection as you remove or "clean" it. Carry a nut pick to help you remove jammed pieces. When you come to an anchor, find a good stance or position and then find the best direction for removing the anchor.

Always clean the protection from the rock to the rope so that anything you accidently drop will remain clipped to the rope. Place any runners over your head and shoulder so these will not droop and snare your feet as you climb.

If you have difficulty removing a piece of gear, you may have to ask the belayer for tension so you can hang from the rope with both hands free. Once the gear is in hand, you can signal the belayer that you are again ready to climb.

Changing Leads

On a long route your rope may run short before the route ends. In such cases, you will need to stop and establish an anchor, then bring up your second before proceeding. When routes are broken into segments like this they are said to be "multipitch," with each segment constituting a "pitch." During multipitch climbs, the climbers usually "swing" leads by exchanging the rack at the belays and leapfrogging. When the second arrives at the next belay, he clips or ties into the anchor system before going "off belay." The gear is reorganized and a careful exchange made. The new leader goes "on belay" and begins the next pitch. It is important to get protection in early on each pitch to prevent a fall directly onto the anchors.

If one climber is doing all of the leading, the rope will have to be restacked between pitches to put the proper end on top of the pile. The gear is collected from the second and organized onto the rack. The belay is then switched back over to the second.

Leading Sport Climbs

Since sport routes have permanently fixed protection, the leader usually can leave the rack behind and carry a selection of quickdraws clipped to her harness. Check the guidebook carefully, however, since some routes will require a traditional gear placement or two.

Many guidebooks will state the exact number of bolts on a given route, so all you need are the necessary number of quickdraws. It is a good idea to carry a couple of extra quickdraws, however, in case you drop one. You will also need a couple of quickdraws, or runners with biners, to clip into the anchors while you rethread the rope to be lowered.

When you come to a bolt, find the best body position for making the clip. Take a quickdraw from your harness and clip it directly into the bolt hanger. Reach down, pull up enough rope to reach the quickdraw, and clip it into the lower biner. On steep rock, you will need to steady the biner with your middle finger and make the clip by grasping the rope between your thumb and index finger.

Be sure to clip the bolt such that the rope end attached to you exits the side of the quickdraw that you will be climbing over. If a fall occurs as you cross laterally over a protection point, the rope can unclip, so plan your clips accordingly!

Sport routes usually end at fixed anchors, which often consist of two or three bolts with or without chain extensions. Open hooks, known as cold shuts, are also common. Once the anchors are attained, the route has been completed.

Cold shuts, "shuts" for short, are convenient in that you can simply flip the rope over the open ends to enable the climber to lower himself to the ground. Beware of top-roping off cold shuts that are not welded to form continuous loops. Some of these open shuts can bend outward and drop the rope under low forces. For the same reason, go slowly and avoid bouncing when lowering off shuts.

The leader's end of the rope should exit the biner on the side she will move past.

If the anchors consist of multiple fixed points, such as bolts with hangers or chains, you will need to clip into the anchors and untie in order to thread the rope through. Clip an independent quickdraw or runner through each anchor and then into your harness, preferably with locking biners. Clip directly into the bolt hangers if possible, or into links of the chain.

Before you untie, pull up some rope and tie a figure-8 knot to clip into your harness waistbelt. Stay on belay! If the anchors blow out while you are untied, the rope will hold you at the next bolt down. This will also protect you from getting stranded should you accidentally drop the rope.

Double-check everything, and if all is well untie from the rope, thread the anchors, and retie into your harness. Untie the safety knot and have the belayer take in all slack and put you on tension. Once you unclip the runners or quickdraws from the anchor, the belayer can lower you to the ground.

The quickdraws on the route can be retrieved as you lower off. Just request "tension" at each point and unclip the quickdraw from the bolt, then from the rope.

SAFETY TIP

Most modern sport routes use strong (3/8" or 1/2") diameter steel bolts and commercial-grade stainless steel hangers. When correctly set, these modern bolts are extremely strong. Some older routes sport rusty 1/4" studs with homemade hangers of unknown quality. Beware of single 1/4" bolts or bolts that are heavily rusted. Bolts that are set crooked or are bent are suspect.

How to Get Down

Getting back to the ground from top-roped or sport routes is fairly straightforward— you are lowered off the top anchors by the belayer. When a safe descent by being lowered is not an option, you must explore other possibilities. Always plan your descent before starting the climb.

Walking Down

The first choice for descent is to walk down over easy terrain. Even the 900-meter "Nose" of El Capitan in Yosemite Valley has a walk-off route from the top. Guidebooks often describe how to find such *walk-offs*. Use caution when you have to bushwhack off-trail, because hidden cliffs and dangerous, exposed slabs often emerge.

Rappelling

When a walk-off is not an option and you cannot lower, you must rappel. Rappelling involves a friction-controlled descent of the rope. It is one of the few instances in free climbing where the anchor and equipment must support your entire weight for an extended period. When rappelling, you must not make mistakes.

First and foremost, you need a strong anchor, or a series of anchors if the route is longer than a rope length. The best rappel anchors are often strong natural features that you can sling with webbing. The rope is doubled and threaded through the webbing loop so it can be pulled and retrieved once you are safely down. The anchor set-up is left behind when rappelling, so artificial anchors are used as a last resort. Make certain that the anchor is sound, for it must support you for the entire rappel. Rappel anchor failures are usually fatal.

Many routes have established rappel anchors threaded with several webbing loops of various qualities left by previous parties. Who knows how long such slings have been exposed to sunlight, the weather, and other destructive forces? Always add a sling of your own to these anchors. You can cut out one or more of the older, most worn slings to make room for the new one, but pack this garbage out and deposit it in a trash can.

Since you must pull the rope through the slings after the rappel, make sure it moves freely and will not bind against the lip of the rock. The rope must not run over any sharp edges, because rappelling often produces a sawing action on the rope.

On long rappels you will need to join two ropes with a grapevine knot to provide a doubled rope. Remember which rope to pull after completing the rappel, so you're not attempting to pull the knot through the sling loop. Tie the free ends of the ropes together with a large knot, or tie large stopper knots into the individual ends, to prevent accidentally rappelling off the end of the rope. It is best to make certain that the ropes will reach the ground or the next set of anchors. If you come up short, you must somehow reascend and locate another route—a strenuous and dangerous proposition involving unprotected hand-over-hand pull-ups or advanced gear techniques.

Look over the rappel route below carefully to determine the best way to get the rope down. In most cases you will coil and toss the rope. Beware of potential snags on trees or bushes. Toss the ropes in sections if necessary.

A figure-8 ring rappel set-up. The quickdraws should be moved from under the rope to avoid abrading the slings during descent. Also, the rope may be passed directly through the anchor sling loop, without the carabiners, as these would be left behind when the rope is retrieved.

You can rappel with your belay device although the friction generated could excessively heat the locking carabiner. The most popular rappel device is the figure-8 ring. A bight of rope is pulled through the large ring of the figure-8 and looped around the stem. The figure-8 ring is then connected to your harness by a locking biner through the small ring. This locks the rope onto the figure-8.

Before beginning the rappel, double-check your harness buckle, the rappel device set-up, the anchor, and the location of the knot if two ropes were joined. You will face into the rock and walk backward down the face during the rappel. Keep your feet slightly spread for balance and sit back on the rope to produce counterpressure for your feet on the rock. Call out "rappelling" loudly to warn anyone below that you are coming down.

Your guide hand is used for balance on the uphill rope while your brake hand controls the speed of descent. With a figure-8 device, the brake hand will increase friction by bending the rope back across your hip. Moving the brake hand out to the side will decrease friction and enable a faster descent. If you need to stop temporarily during a rappel, apply a hand brake, then wrap the rope around one leg several times as a friction brake.

SAFETY TIPS

Walk slowly down the rock when rappelling to avoid extreme heat buildup due to friction. Avoid bounding and sideward movements, as these increase the sawing action of the rope against the lip of the rock near the anchor. Tie back any loose clothing, hair, helmet straps, and gear to avoid these getting sucked into the figure-8 ring and jamming the rope. Such jams are almost always impossible for the rappeller to clear without help and a sharp knife.

Retrieving the Rope

When you are safely on the ground or connected to a secure anchor at the end of the rappel, you can disconnect your figure-8 ring from the rope. Before retrieving the rope, make sure it is free from any knots or tangles and that you will be pulling the correct end. If you are on the ground or on a huge ledge, it may help to walk the ends of the rope a few steps away from the cliff face; this makes it easier to pull. Pull the rope steadily and shout "rope!" when it pulls free of the anchors.

4

ROCK CLIMBING FITNESS AND SAFETY

The classic image of rock climbing is a large, heavily muscled male cranking a series of one-arm pull-ups to the top of the crag. Experience has taught me that this image is flawed. I have seen individuals unable to complete one pull-up in the gym who can dance up the rock with little appearance of serious effort. An attuned sense of balance and using your legs to "press" your body upward, rather than strenuous pulling with your arms, are the keys to efficient rock climbing.

Of course, routes with radical overhangs and those that require long reaches and pulls with the arms demand more muscular strength and endurance. Eventually, you will progress to the point at which you must consider specific training and conditioning. Initially, however, you can select routes that are the most user-friendly given your current level of fitness. Climbing areas typically offer a wide variety of routes at all difficulty levels. Thus, everyone in the group can find an adequately challenging route, making for an enjoyable day.

Preparing to Climb

The passage from the car to the crux of the climb may prove a rude awakening for your body. Before you tie in to the rope and confront the route, you should perform some warm-up activities. The basic warm-up should include a sequence of 10 to 15 minutes of aerobic activity followed by stretching and easy bouldering.

The access hike from the parking lot to the rock often serves as a good aerobic warm-up. It's funny how the crag is often at the top of an extended, moderately steep hillside! This brief period of aerobic activity often helps to settle your nerves a bit as well. Ten to 15 minutes of aerobic warm-up will increase the temperature and blood flow in your muscles, preparing them for the climb.

A series of stretching exercises for the upper and lower body will help increase your range of motion and likely improve your reach for those distant holds. Some experts feel that stretching before exercise helps prevent injury to muscles and connective tissues around the joints.

Warm-up Stretches

After the brief aerobic warm-up, perform a series of stretches for the major muscle groups. Begin each stretch by moving gradually to the point of slight tension. Avoid stretches that cause pain. Hold each stretch for 15 to 20 seconds, then release the tension, relax, and repeat. Keep breathing in a regular pattern. Repeat each exercise with the opposite side of the body when indicated.

ELBOW PULL-ACROSS

Raise an arm above your head, then bend the elbow to place your hand down your back. With the passive hand, pull the bent elbow across your midline to stretch the shoulder. You can add a torso bend to the side to stretch the lateral back.

ELBOW PULL-ACROSS

FOREARM TWISTER

This stretch is great for your wrists, forearms, and upper back. Extend one arm in front with the palm up. Place the elbow of the opposite arm in the crook of the extended arm. Flex the extended arm toward you and rotate this palm to place the fingers in the opposite palm. Now push outward, away from your chest to the point of tension.

FOREARM TWISTER

TORSO TWIST In a seated position, extend one leg and cross the other over it at the knee. Using arm pressure against the upper knee, twist your shoulders away from the extended leg. Continue the stretch through the neck by looking back over your shoulder.

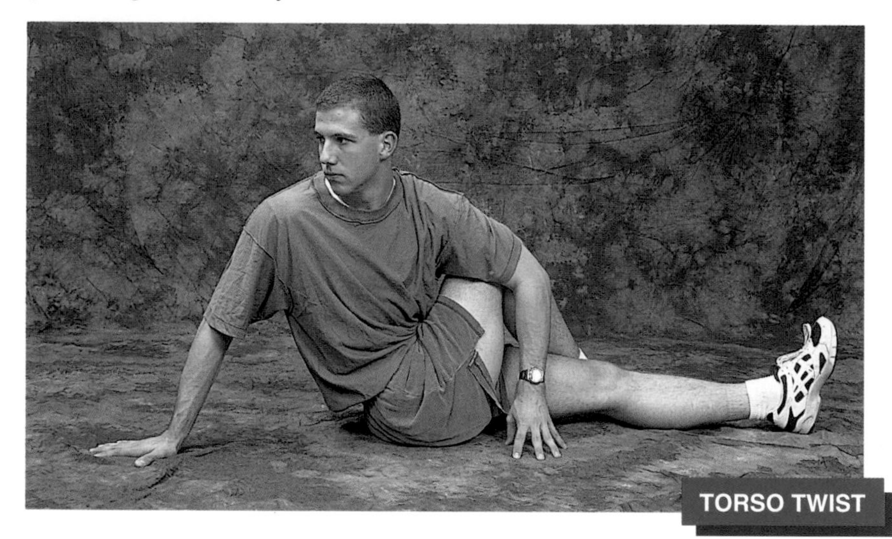

TORSO TWIST

HAMSTRING STRETCH Extend one leg forward and bend the opposite leg at the knee to place the sole of the foot against the thigh. Slowly bend forward to slide your arms down the extended leg.

HAMSTRING STRETCH

TURNOUTS This stretch will get you ready for thin moves on vertical rock. From a lying position with your spine straight and your lower back on the ground, place the soles of your feet together and allow gravity to pull your knees open.

TURNOUTS

BIG-STEPS From a kneeling position, extend one leg backwards with the knee touching the ground. Position the opposite leg forward with the sole of the foot on the ground and the knee flexed but behind the ankle. Using your arms for balance, lower the thigh of the rear leg toward the ground. As your flexibility increases, you can stretch the forward foot further ahead of the knee.

BIG-STEPS

Warm-up Bouldering

Follow your stretching with a period of easy bouldering. This will provide a climbing-specific warm-up and attune you to the rock. Begin by simply walking along the ground at the base of the rock as you grasp and pull easily on holds. Take it easy, and practice side-pulls and underclings as well as regular cling grips.

Gradually step up onto the rock and traverse it, using shuffle steps and cross-overs. Use large footholds to avoid overstressing the arms and fingers. Be relaxed, breathe easily, and practice resting. Use a spotter if you need one.

Developing Climbing-Specific Fitness

If you climb on a regular basis, your fitness will gradually begin to develop. However, you will progress faster and enjoy a greater volume of climbing by doing some specific training. A regular program of exercise is particularly important for the off-season and for those individuals who can only get to the rock occasionally.

Improving Muscular Strength and Endurance

A generic program of resistance exercise, or weightlifting, designed for overall muscle fitness can go a long way toward improving your performance on the rock. However, most climbers agree that maximum benefits are obtained from climbing-specific exercise.

On the Rocks

Bouldering remains the mainstay of specific muscle development for climbing. Workouts can be tailored to develop strength, endurance, or technique. To build strength and power, perform several repetitions of a difficult movement sequence, four to eight single moves, with up to five minutes of rest between repetitions.

Long routes, or difficult routes that require significant problem-solving time demand a high level of endurance. You can build endurance through bouldering by staying on the rock for a designated time period, such as 10 minutes, and increasing the time to 15 to 20 minutes as you improve. Move to a new handhold or foothold every 5 to 10 seconds, and vary movement from horizontal traverses to vertical moves and downclimbs.

You can use bouldering games to provide variety, motivation, and development of technical skills. Some of my favorites are:

- **nose-touch**—Every time you change to a different handhold, you must touch your nose to the back of that hand before the next move. This game will also help develop your sense of weight transfer and balance as you position for the nose-touches.

- **all holds**—Designate a section of rock to explore and use as many holds as possible before coming down.
- **add-on**—You and a partner agree upon three holds to use to mount the rock. You then take turns selecting and using two new holds to extend the route. If you fall before completing the sequence of moves currently in the game, you must start again at the beginning.
- **slo-mo**—Work through both easy and difficult problems in slow motion. This will help develop precise hand and foot placements and tune you in to weight transfer.
- **one-foot off**—Make every move to a new handhold with one foot off the rock. This will help you develop the ability to "flag" a leg for counter-balance and increase the load on the arms for greater resistance.

Training with a Hangboard

If you can't get out to the rock to boulder, or weather is bad, a hangboard can provide a good climbing-specific workout. Hangboards are manufactured with sculpted holds that simulate actual rock holds and textures. You can also design and construct a hangboard out of wood, using blocks for edges and drilled holes for pockets. Use a sander to round off any sharp edges that might cause tendon strain in your fingers.

Hangboard workouts typically involve static hangs on a variety of hold contours and pull-up moves on medium to large holds. If you are not yet strong enough to do a full two-arm pull-up, prop your legs on a chair or ladder to relieve some of your weight.

Ten-minute sequences are popular for hangboard workouts. A set of 10 exercises are identified, and the climber has 60 seconds to complete each exercise and rest before moving to the next exercise. At first, one complete 10-minute sequence will constitute a workout; however, you can work up to three sequences, with 5 to 10 minutes of rest between each. With time and improvement, you may intensify your workout by increasing the number of pull-ups, using smaller holds, or adding resistance with a weighted belt or vest. Here is a sample 10-minute sequence:

1. 5 double-arm pull-ups on large holds.
2. 10-second hang on large holds + 3 pull-ups on pockets.
3. 10-second hang on small holds + 2 pull-ups on pockets.
4. 10-second hang on pockets + 3 pull-ups on large holds.
5. 15-second hang on large holds.
6. 10-second hang on large holds + 2 pull-ups on small holds.

7. 3 pull-ups on large holds + 3 pull-ups on pockets.
8. 10-second hang on large holds + 2 pull-ups on pockets.
9. 20-second hang on large holds + 2 pull-ups on large holds.
10. Maximum hang on large holds.

A hangboard can provide climbing-specific training when resources and space are limited.

SAFETY TIPS

You should limit strenuous, strength-building workouts to two or three a week. Climbing-specific exercises can quickly lead to injured tendons in your fingers or hands if you don't rest between workouts. When training with added resistance, such as a weighted vest, use fairly large holds and be particularly wary of overstrain in your hands and fingers.

Developing Cardiorespiratory Fitness

Cardiorespiratory exercise is *aerobic*, which means that energy expenditure occurs in the presence of oxygen. Aerobic exercise conditions the pulmonary and circulatory systems and improves overall endurance.

Studies conducted in the United States and France have observed aerobic energy expenditure rates of between 8 and 11 kilocalories per minute during sustained difficult climbing. These energy rates are approximately seven to eight times a resting adult's average energy expenditure. Although the time required to complete a one-pitch route is relatively brief, an ongoing program of cardiorespiratory fitness will help you battle fatigue.

You needn't train like a marathon runner to develop adequate aerobic fitness for rock climbing. A basic program that involves sustained total-body activity, such as walking, jogging, cycling, and swimming, performed for 20 minutes or more 3 to 5 days per week, should be adequate. Cross-country skiing and hiking with ski poles provide excellent conditioning and involve the arms and upper body to a greater degree.

If you have not performed such exercise in a while, begin gradually with shorter sessions. As your fitness improves, increase the intensity and duration of your workouts. If you experience any unusual symptoms, such as dizziness, persistent pain in the chest or arms, or lingering muscle or joint discomfort, consult your physician.

The Effect of Body Composition

Overall body composition is described in two categories: fat-free weight, which includes the skeleton, organs, and muscle tissues; and body fat, which includes essential fat and stored adipose fat. Excess storage fat will work against you in rock climbing. Any excess weight adds to the forces imposed on your arms and fingers and increases the resistance that must be lifted in pull-up moves.

Research on the anthropometry (body type and build) of world-class rock climbers, both male and female, has found that, although these athletes did not possess unusually high absolute strength, their strength-to-weight ratios (strength per pound of body weight) were at the top of the scale. Body composition analyses in this study indicated that much of the favorable strength-to-weight ratio was due to low relative body fat.

While leanness may provide advantages in rock climbing, there are some indications that extreme reductions in body fat are associated with loss of strength and potentially serious metabolic problems. There is a balance; the better climbers maintain nutrition through low-fat diets similar to those followed by distance runners and other aerobic athletes.

Strictly dieting to restrict your calorie intake, and thus reduce body fat, results in a considerable loss of muscle protein. A regular exercise program that combines aerobic activity with strength-building and endurance exercise is the best way to burn excess calories and maintain lean tissues.

PROBLEM SOLVING ON THE EDGE

Climbing is about movement and problem solving. Although physical fitness is important, there is more to the game. Much of climbing involves one's ability to sense the rock through touch and vision, interpret these sensations, and produce the positions and movements necessary to proceed.

The best way to develop problem-solving skills is to work on unfamiliar moves and routes. As you repeat a given move, your nervous system begins to store the required signals that activate the muscles in a coordinated manner. It is a well-known phenomenon that a difficult boulder problem or sequence of moves begins to feel easier with practice. The more unique problems you solve, the greater your repertory of climbing moves.

Cruising familiar routes is fun, but you should spend some time working on new and difficult problems. Low-key competitive bouldering sessions, where one climber secretly works out a problem then presents it as a challenge to another, can be quite valuable. Avoid asking for beta (information about the route) until you have attempted it unsuccessfully several times.

Fear of heights and fear of falling are two of the most significant barriers to the development of problem-solving skills. Anxiety can not only inhibit you from trying difficult moves, but also can scramble the appropriate neuromuscular signals that are necessary for smooth, efficient movement.

Spend some time on the rope learning to trust the gear and belays. Expect to take some falls when you are pushing your limits. Just make certain that the safety system is intact and working!

Indoor Climbing Walls

Modern indoor artificial walls and gymnasiums are good places to work on problems that are above your ability. The routes are usually short, and the abundance of modular holds on the walls allows countless variations and problem designs.

© Cheyenne Rouse

Sport leading on an indoor climbing wall.

Indoor climbing walls are fun to play on and provide a great social atmosphere for sharing techniques and stories about your latest adventures. Rehearsing countless difficult techniques in nearly complete safety will rapidly develop your climbing skills.

However, be cautious of overstrain when climbing in the gym. It is easy to expose muscles and tendons too much, too quickly. Also, the relative safety of artificial walls can lead to carelessness when climbing outdoors on real rock: Be aware that the environments are not the same.

Dressing for the Rock

The one guiding principle on how to dress for rock climbing is movement! Dress in clothing that enables great freedom of movement. Shorts and a T-shirt or tank-top are the traditional mainstays. Avoid extremely loose or floppy clothes that could get caught in the rope or anchors.

Lycra tights are comfortable and do not block your view of your feet when you are struggling for purchase on tiny edges. For climbs on abrasive rock, you might consider long pants made of durable materials.

Be prepared for weather changes. On multipitch routes you should consider carrying a small pack with a hooded rain jacket, hat, and a warm shirt or sweater for your upper body.

Objective Hazards

You can control many aspects of risk in climbing, such as the anchor set-up, quality of belay techniques, and age and status of equipment. However, there are factors inherent in the activity over which you have little control. Such factors are called objective hazards and primarily involve environmental risks.

Rockfall

The outdoor climbing environment is an ever-changing arena in which events are often unpredictable. Rockfall constitutes one of the primary objective hazards for the climber. A hiker, other climber, or animal at the top of the crag can dislodge debris. Sometimes a climber or the rope will loosen rocks; sometimes the stones just fall. A helmet provides some protection, but don't ask for trouble by climbing on poor rock or below obvious hazards such as discharge gullies. Be especially careful not to dislodge rocks when others are below you or while you are setting up top-rope anchors.

Holds can break off anytime, even on the most solid rock. Sandstone is particularly friable after rains. When a hold breaks, a climber often falls with the loose rock. This is a major reason to avoid free soloing—all your climbing skill is useless when you are zipping through the air grasping a broken hold.

Weather

Weather, too, can be a major problem. On short routes and top-rope climbs, a cold rain or sudden snowshower may be no more than a nuisance that marks the end of the climbing day. In contrast, on long, multipitch routes or in mountaineering, escape may require several involved rappels—if it's possible at all.

Lightning is a very real and immediate danger. I remember getting caught on a pinnacle in Colorado in a sudden storm which boomed and flashed all around as we quickly rappelled off. Later we heard that two climbers were struck by lightning high on a route less than a half-mile away. Be familiar with local weather patterns, and rest on those days when it looks stormy.

Plants and Animals

Flora and fauna also pose objective hazards. The bases of many rock crags are adorned with poison ivy and poison oak. Learn to recognize and avoid these plants. I have run into hornets and wasps, rattlesnakes, bats, and even frogs on various cliff faces. Rousing a pigeon from an alcove can be a significant fright that leads to a long fall.

SAFETY TIP

Assemble a first-aid kit to include with your gear. It is essential to include a selection of Band-Aids, trauma dressings and bandages, butterfly closure strips, athletic tape, wound-cleansing preparations, and analgesic tablets. Additional helpful items include a blister repair kit, antibiotic ointment, tweezers, sunscreen, insect repellent, and latex gloves. Treatments for specific allergies, such as bee stings, should be included. Nail clippers and a small emery board are invaluable for trimming cracked fingernails. Toss in a sharp camping knife for cutting webbing and cord to rig emergency anchors and rappels. Before you leave home, locate the closest emergency services in the climbing area.

EARTH WATCH

Access to the rock is a growing problem for climbers on both public and private lands. As rock climbing becomes more popular and the crags more crowded, the impact becomes more serious. It is very important that we take care of these wonderful resources.

- Keep climbing areas clean—do not litter. Always dispose of trash you encounter along the way.
- Use established trails and participate actively in trail-building and maintenance projects.
- Do not destroy the rock with hammers or graffiti. Be kind to the surrounding vegetation.
- Use chalk sparingly. Tie loose chalk into an old, thin sock and keep it in your chalkbag. This encourages you to ration out your chalk.
- Request access permission from landowners and respect no-trespassing signs.

5

THE BEST PLACES TO ROCK CLIMB

If you live near mountainous terrain, finding good local rock climbing will not likely be a problem. You can climb every weekend and probably never exhaust the area. The combination of fun moves high in the mountain air is satisfaction enough.

However, if you don't have a view of the Rockies from your kitchen window, don't despair. Boulders and crags are usually not too far away. In my home area, along the shore of Lake Superior in upper Michigan, the highest point of land is just over 300 meters above sea level. With the normal water level of Lake Superior at 180 meters, there's not much relief in the terrain. Still, the crags are out there, nestled into the north woods and particularly along the shoreline of the big lake.

My family and several climber-friends enjoy taking climbing vacations. In winter, when snow covers everything at home, we explore maps and guidebooks and dream of warm, sunny rock. Once our destination has been identified, we gather information about the local history, geography, and natural environment of the area. Pre-planning saves us a lot of time: When we finally arrive, we're ready for the rock. When the actual trip is over, we take home not only memories of the rock and routes, but an enhanced appreciation of our beautiful planet.

Professional guide services are good sources of information and can provide complete outfitted excursions for all climbers, beginner to advanced. Many of the larger population centers and university communities have organized climbing clubs, which often offer instruction and activities at which you can meet potential climbing partners.

ABOUT CLIMBING GUIDEBOOKS

Guidebooks are your main source of information, and virtually every established area has at least one published reference. Mini-guides are usually published in popular climbing/mountaineering magazines and present condensed versions of the main guides.

The guidebook to an area usually contains access information and maps of the rocks. Individual climbing routes are depicted on photographs or drawings to make location and identification easy. Some guides provide detailed diagrams, or *topos*, of the more popular or classic routes.

As a minimum, the name and difficulty rating for each established route is presented. Most guides also provide a quality rating, usually via a series of stars, and information concerning the availability of protection points for leading the route. Modern guidebooks may list the length of a route, so you will know whether an extra rope is required for the rappel off the top.

Other useful information that appears in most guidebooks includes listings of motels and campgrounds where you can stay during your visit, good places to eat and shop, and emergency service locations and phone numbers. Climbing history and some environmental information are common as well.

United States Getaways

The geological diversity of the United States provides a vast array of rock types and moods for climbing. Variations in seasonal climates enable serious climbers to travel from area to area and crank rock in good weather all year round. No matter when you take your vacation, there is a major climbing area waiting for you in the United States. A mere sample is presented here.

Yosemite National Park, California

Yosemite Valley is one of the most famous rock-climbing areas in the world. As you enter the Valley along the Merced River, the vaulted heights and sheer volume of rock is astounding. Historically, Yosemite has inspired the best mountaineers from all over the world, and it remains a must for aspiring climbers.

Don't let the *Big Walls*, like the sheer 600-meter Northwest Face of Half Dome, intimidate you. There are many high-quality routes to savor that are shorter and easier. Take a look at *The Grack* on Glacier Point Apron, a three-star, four-pitch route rated at 5.6.

While the walls of the Valley are impressive, the neighboring area of Tuolumne Meadows is unmatched in beauty. Dazzling granite domes of all sizes spring from lush meadows just a few yards from your car. The higher elevation of Tuolumne provides cool relief from the sweltering summer heat of the Valley.

The easier routes in Tuolumne often sport bold runouts on smooth granite, and the bolted sport climbs are tough. The sheer volume of rock, however, yields something for everyone. My six-year-old daughter danced up three friction routes on one roadside slab, to the applause of surprised tourists below.

Joshua Tree National Park, California

When other areas suffer from unstable weather, Joshua Tree comes into its own. The best periods to visit this high desert area in Southern California are October through December and March through April. The rock is quartz monzonite, a rough, abrasive type of granite that takes the form of domes and boulders scattered among open plains.

Josh is primarily a traditional lead-climbing and bouldering area, but many sport routes are scattered about. The area is extensive, to say the least. The most recent guidebook lists thousands of routes and boulder problems, rated from 5.0 to 5.13d.

Smith Rock, Oregon

Originally a little used traditional climbing area, Smith Rock vaulted to one of the world's foremost sport crags in the 1980s. Actually a grouping of several crags within a canyon of the Crooked River, this area presents hundreds of routes at all difficulty levels. The beauty of the canyon and the view of the snow-capped Three Sisters Mountains in the distance make Smith a scenic visit as well.

The rock at Smith is welded tuff, volcanic in origin, and often contains fragments of rhyolite, called xenoliths, that present unique knobs and excellent face-climbing holds. In addition, there are often remnants of vesicles that form fingertip- to bathtub-sized pockets.

There are many traditional lead routes at Smith, but this area contains some of the best fully bolted sport climbs around; even routes in the lower grades like *Bunny Face* at 5.7. The current (1995) most difficult route in the United States, *Just Do It* (5.14d), is located on the astounding Monkey Face formation at Smith Rock.

Exposed climbing high on the Monkey Face formation at Smith Rock, Oregon.

Red Rocks, Nevada

Just 15 miles west of glittering Las Vegas lies a multicolored escarpment cut by many canyons and undulations that offers over 1,000 routes to the climber. This is the Red Rock Canyon National Conservation Area, or Red Rocks for short.

The Red Rocks contain everything from powerful, bolted sport routes to 10+ pitch traditional leads. The rock is Aztec sandstone, beautifully swirled in cream, pink, and lavender shades that appear to leap from the surrounding desert. You can climb year-round at the Red Rocks; however, summer temperatures can zoom to well over 100 degrees Fahrenheit by afternoon.

Boulder, Colorado

The volume of good rock around Boulder is so vast that it takes several guidebooks just to present information on the most noted crags. The rich climbing history of the area means that quality traditional routes abound, and the overall volume and quality of rock means that there are many sport routes as well.

The 300-meter East Face of the Third Flatiron, at 5.2 to 5.3, is one of the longest and most exposed easy routes in the country. Some of the pitches are runout with long distances between protection points, but the belays have bombproof eyebolts to tie off. Fun moves, breathtaking positions, and a grand summit view make the East Face a classic.

With the conglomerate sandstone of the Flatirons, the solid granite of Boulder Canyon, and the steep, tight walls of Eldorado Canyon, Boulder has it all. When you have cranked your fill and need a day of rest, numerous hiking trails provide a relaxed diversion.

Hueco Tanks, Texas

Lead climbs, top-ropes, and a wealth of world-class bouldering are the lures of Hueco Tanks. The area gets its name from the narrow-lipped pockets, or *huecos*, that dot the rock.

Just a short distance east of El Paso, Hueco Tanks is a prime winter destination for climbers from around the world. Although it can be cool at night, the rock warms quickly, and rain is almost nonexistent.

Devil's Tower National Monument, Wyoming

Probably no other rock formation in the United States stirs the imagination like Devil's Tower. The Tower is composed of large four- to six-sided volcanic columns that make for steep profiles on all sides. The easiest route to the summit of Devil's Tower is rated at 5.6, and the crux moves on the second pitch may seem harder. The surrounding prairie lands and twisted Belle Fourche River provide calm contrasts to the Tower's steepness.

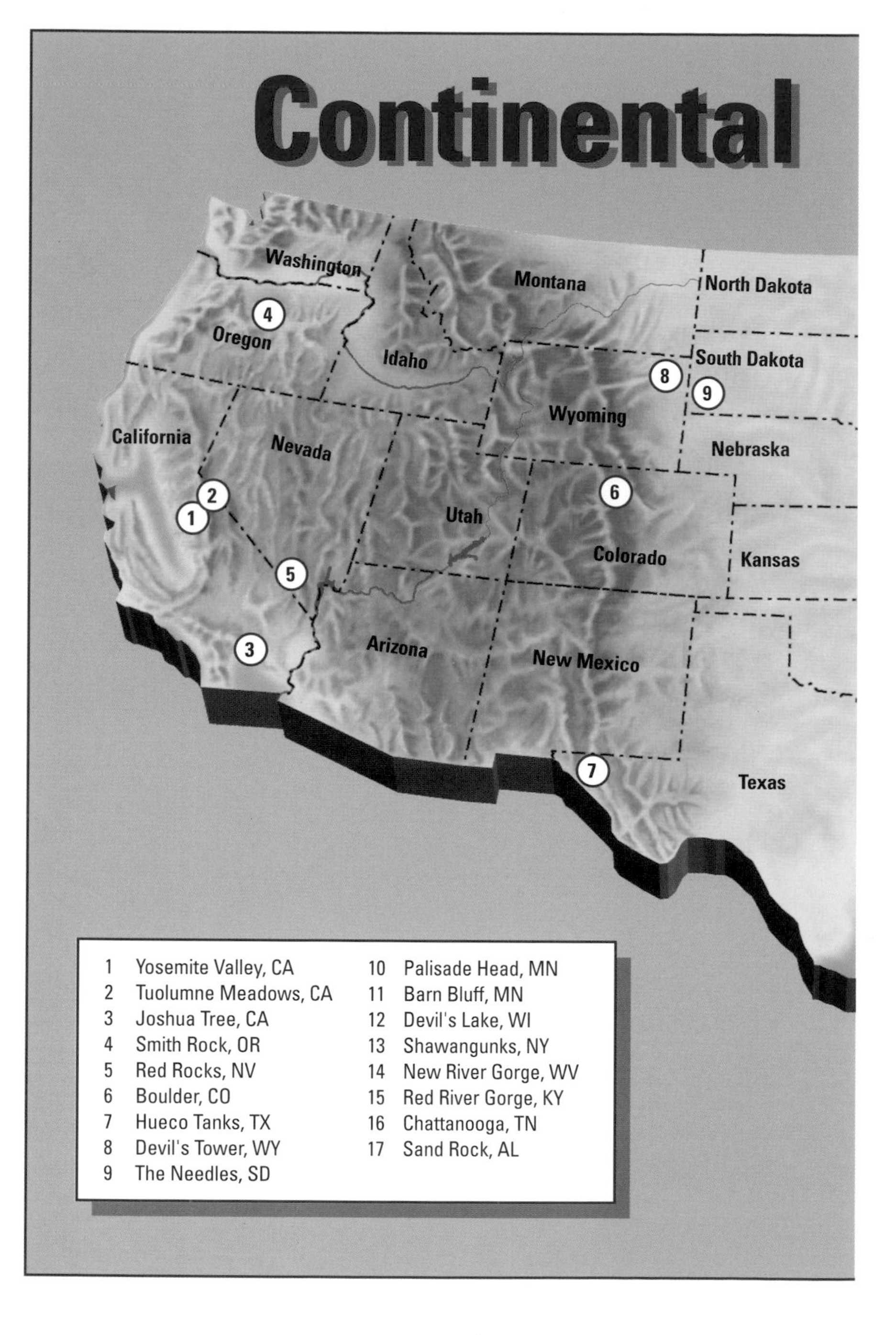
Continental
Washington
Montana
North Dakota
Oregon
Idaho
South Dakota
Wyoming
California
Nevada
Nebraska
Utah
Colorado
Kansas
Arizona
New Mexico
Texas
1 Yosemite Valley, CA
2 Tuolumne Meadows, CA
3 Joshua Tree, CA
4 Smith Rock, OR
5 Red Rocks, NV
6 Boulder, CO
7 Hueco Tanks, TX
8 Devil's Tower, WY
9 The Needles, SD
10 Palisade Head, MN
11 Barn Bluff, MN
12 Devil's Lake, WI
13 Shawangunks, NY
14 New River Gorge, WV
15 Red River Gorge, KY
16 Chattanooga, TN
17 Sand Rock, AL

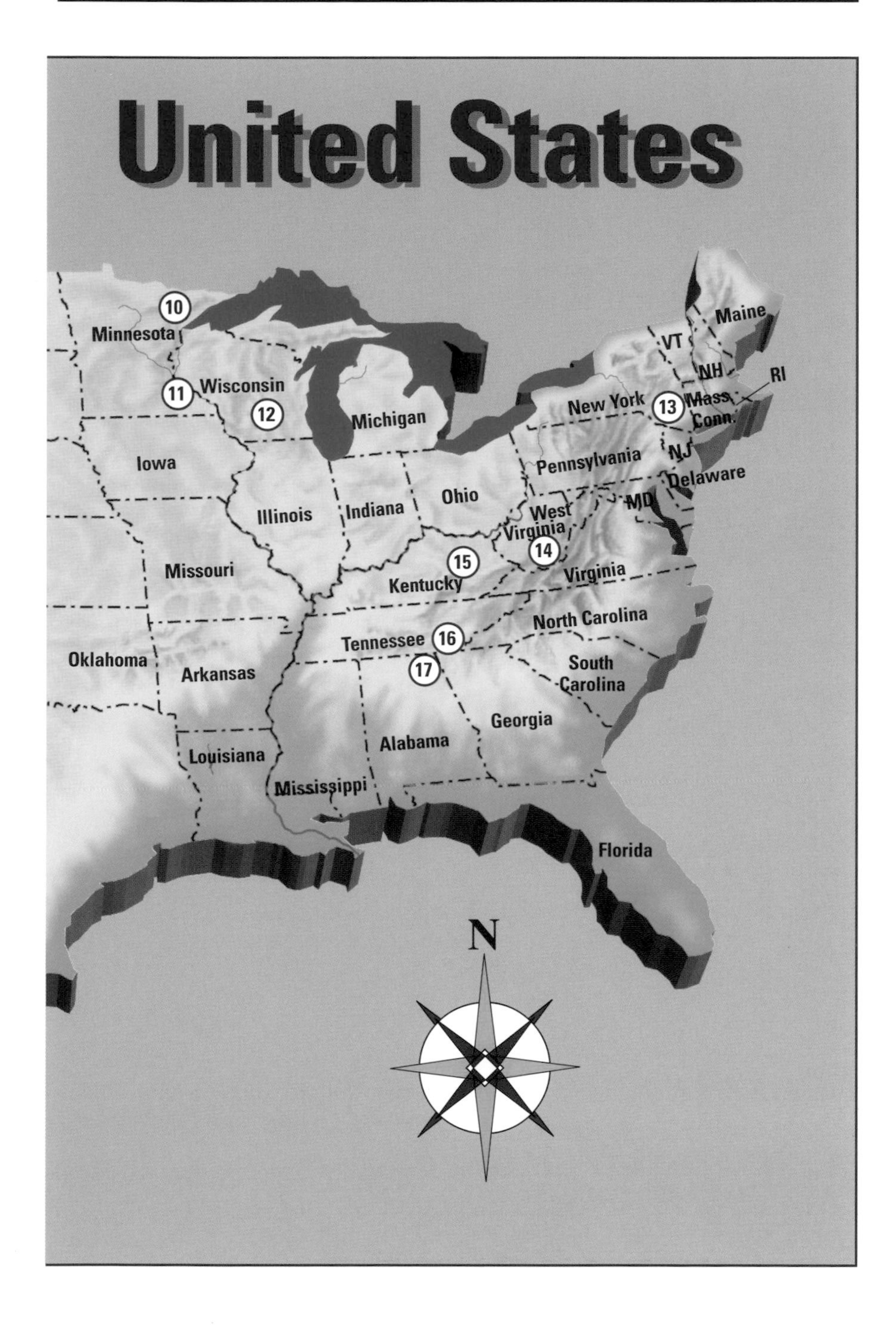
United States
Minnesota
Wisconsin
Michigan
Iowa
Illinois
Indiana
Ohio
Missouri
Kentucky
Tennessee
Oklahoma
Arkansas
Louisiana
Mississippi
Alabama
Georgia
Florida
South Carolina
North Carolina
Virginia
West Virginia
Pennsylvania
New York
Maine
VT
NH
Mass.
RI
Conn.
NJ
Delaware
MD
10
11
12
13
14
15
16
17
N

Crack climbs abound, but there are also big-time stemming moves between columns, like on the classic *El Matador* (5.10d). Some routes venture up the column faces. There are few bolted sport routes at Devil's Tower so bring a full rack of gear. You will also need two ropes for the series of rappels from the summit.

The Needles, South Dakota

The Needles are found in the Black Hills and are informally divided into two regions. The blocks and spires around Sylvan Lake and the Needles Highway present intimidating face and crack routes, often on airy spires with minimal protection. In contrast, the routes on formations close to the Mt. Rushmore monument tend to be more sporty, with well bolted leads.

The Black Hills are beautiful and the rock quality is usually very good, making the area worth a visit. Don't miss the fun and wild positions for photos on *The Gossamer* (5.8), a wafer-like fin in the Mt. Rushmore area.

Great Lakes Region

The upper Midwest contains several small but beautiful areas with much to offer. Along the north shore of Lake Superior in Minnesota are a number of high-quality basaltic crags. The two showpieces are Palisade Head and Shovel Point, both of which rise directly out of Lake Superior. Imagine working out thin edging moves with a sunny breeze whipping about and the blue waters of the largest body of fresh water in the world spread below.

Most routes can be top-roped with upper belays, but you have to lower off the edge to get to the starts. Local climbers have designated these cliffs as no-chalk areas, so be sensitive to this and leave the chalkbag in the car.

Just southeast of Minneapolis/St. Paul, Minnesota, in the town of Red Wing, is Barn Bluff, a small but significant sport crag. The rock is a type of dolomite limestone that tends toward being vertical to overhanging. Most routes are short and well equipped with bolts.

Inconspicuous in the heart of southern Wisconsin is a real jewel—Devil's Lake State Park. The one-mile long clearwater lake is surrounded by 150-meter talus bluffs, which support extensive pink and purple quartzite crags. This is another beautiful place to hang out, and a cool dip in the lake can be refreshing after a day on the rock.

The routes at Devil's Lake are short, 6 to 21 meters, but the steepness and intensity make up for it. Most climbers top-rope from easy set-ups, but there are some good cracks for leading. There are no bolted sport routes, so you need to bring a rack. Long webbing slings are the standard for tying off trees and blocks to top-rope.

Devil's Lake sports several hundred quality routes with difficulties ranging from 5.0 to 5.13. Although the local area is somewhat rural, Devil's Lake is close to several major population centers and can be very crowded on summer weekends.

The Shawangunks, New York State

The Shawangunks ("Gunks" for short) are another area rich in climbing lore. The rock is a white quartz conglomerate famed for its horizontal holds and overhanging roofs. The Gunks are actually several separate cliffs containing more than 1,000 routes at all difficulty grades. Although just 145 kilometers (90 miles) west of the urban hustle of New York City, the Shawangunks are nestled amid serene, forested hills. The exposure high on the crags above the forest is dramatic and makes for breathtaking photographs.

New River Gorge, West Virginia

The *Endless Wall* high above the river presents a four-mile, continuous length of quality sandstone, and this is just one of the main areas of the "New." The current list of established climbs here totals over 1,200, rated 5.4 to 5.13, with a good mix of traditional and sport routes. The region is truly wild and wonderful, offering additional opportunities for hiking, mountain bicycling, and whitewater river rafting.

Not far to the north stands Seneca Rock, a thin, vertical quartzite fin with routes up to four pitches in length. Climbing at Seneca has a longer history than the New River Gorge, and most routes require traditional gear. Steep routes with big-time exposure characterize the climbing here. Sitting atop the South Peak summit may have you wondering how the thing has kept standing all these years. With all of it's verticality and exposure, Seneca has several classic easy (5.1-5.6) routes to the summits.

Red River Gorge, Kentucky

Here is another extensive sandstone area of the Eastern Appalachian Mountains. Throughout the 1980s the Gorge was primarily a traditional lead climbing area. The 1990s ushered in modern bolting methods, and the quantity of difficult overhanging sport routes skyrocketed.

The Red River Gorge can be quite humid during summer, but fall is outstanding and many winter days offer climbable conditions. The cliffs rise to 61 meters though most routes are less than 24 meters.

Chattanooga, Tennessee

The Chattanooga area in southeastern Tennessee sports several crags and walls of high-quality sandstone that is easy on the hands. The volume of rock is more than adequate to keep you busy for a long time.

Sunset Park, Suck Creek Canyon, and the extensive *Tennessee Wall* are within minutes of downtown. Less than an hour drive to the west is Foster Falls, a scenic gorge with an abundance of bolted routes ranging from 5.5 to 5.13. A bit further to the north is Buzzard Point, where fine sandstone cranking combines with spectacular views.

If you find the steep walls around Chattanooga intimidating, head south to Sand Rock, a short distance off Interstate Highway 59 in northeastern Alabama. Here is a scenic labyrinth of quality sandstone that can be top-roped, led, or bouldered. Sand Rock is touted as one of the best areas in the south for beginning rock climbers, but routes like *Champagne Jam* (5.12c/d) will also entertain the most experienced craggers.

Canadian Climbing

Although noted primarily for big Alpine mountaineering challenges, Canada offers some fine rock cragging as well. Most areas provide relief from the summer heat of more southerly locations.

Squamish, British Columbia

The drive northward along Howe Sound from Vancouver to the town of Squamish is scenic, to say the least. Beyond Squamish lies an outstanding wilderness of forest, meadows, and glaciated mountains. Along the way are numerous rock crags—from the short top-ropes of Lighthouse Park, in West Vancouver to the 600-meter walls of The Chief, dominating the sky above Squamish.

This is granite country, offering long crack lines and some of the most sustained liebacking you could wish for. Try the ample face routes and overhangs. The Apron area of The Chief dishes up some long friction slabs that stretch the rope out for up to seven pitches.

Rest days can involve beautiful Alpine hiking in Garibaldi Provincial Park, windsurfing in the Squamish River estuary, or mountain biking on a forest road. Vancouver offers more cultural diversions, such as art galleries, museums, and marketplaces.

Bow Valley, Alberta

Excellent limestone rock climbing is found within Banff National Park and eastward toward Calgary. One fine crag is found at scenic Lake Louise, north of the town of Banff. Follow the initially paved lakeshore trail from the Chateau to the backside of the lake, with the ice-clad face of Mt. Victoria high above. Most of the routes are bolted.

Many additional peaks and crags rise along the Trans-Canada Highway

(Highway 1) from Banff to Yamnuska to the east. Summer is the best time to visit these areas.

A good spot for short sport climbs is Grotto Canyon, across Highway 1A from Lac des Arcs. The climbs range from delicate slabs to steep edging routes on excellent rock.

© Greg Epperson

Thin limestone climbing above Lake Louise, Alberta, Canada.

The Niagara Escarpment, Ontario

If you are looking for exposed, scenic climbing on solid 400-million-year old limestone, this is the place. The rock is actually dolostone or sedimentary limestone in which some of the calcium has been replaced by magnesium. The escarpment stretches from Niagara Falls through the Bruce Peninsula, which defines the southwest margin of Georgian Bay in Lake Huron. There are several climbing areas along the route.

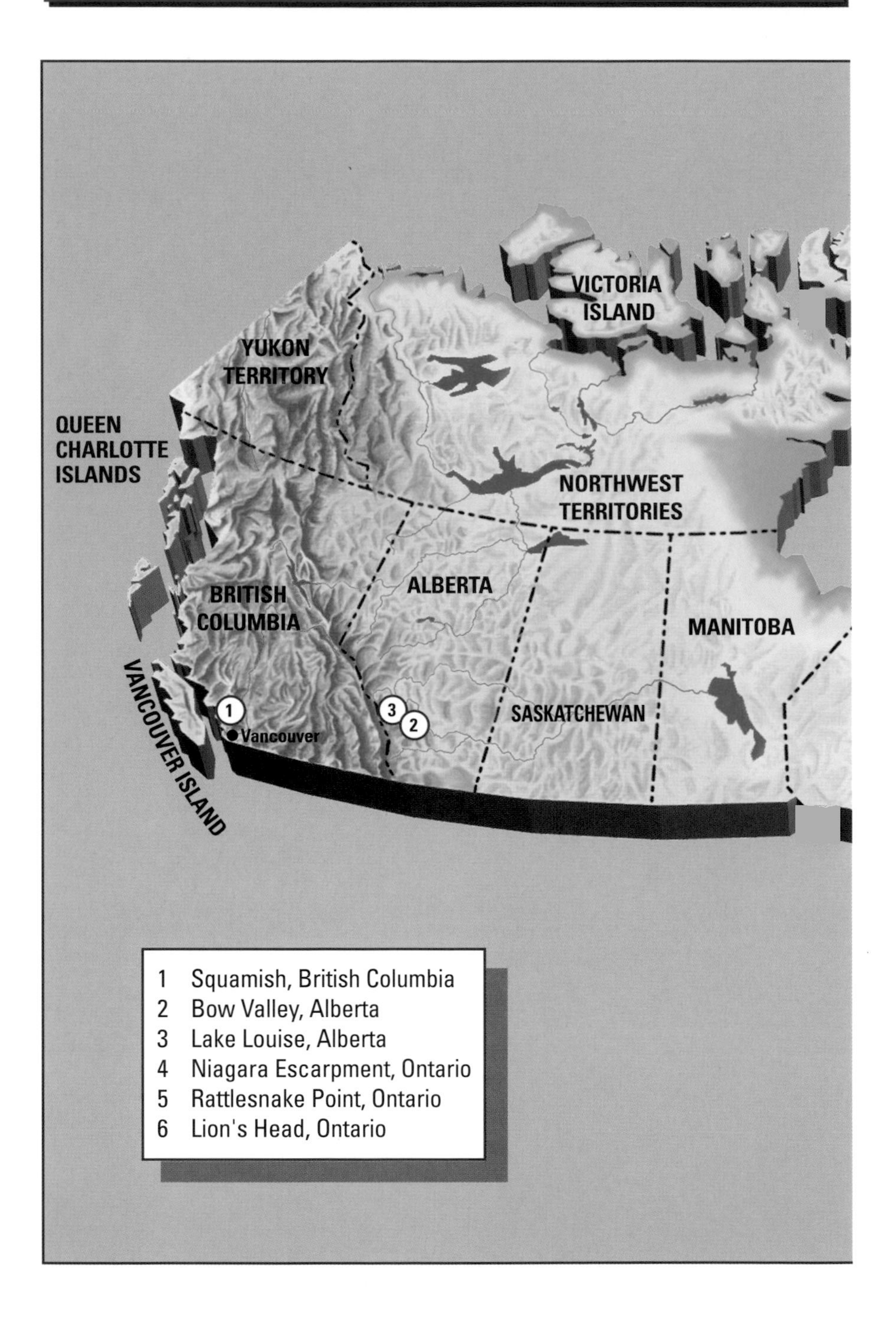
VICTORIA
ISLAND
YUKON
TERRITORY
QUEEN
CHARLOTTE
ISLANDS
NORTHWEST
TERRITORIES
ALBERTA
BRITISH
COLUMBIA
MANITOBA
VANCOUVER ISLAND
1
Vancouver
3
2
SASKATCHEWAN
1 Squamish, British Columbia
2 Bow Valley, Alberta
3 Lake Louise, Alberta
4 Niagara Escarpment, Ontario
5 Rattlesnake Point, Ontario
6 Lion's Head, Ontario

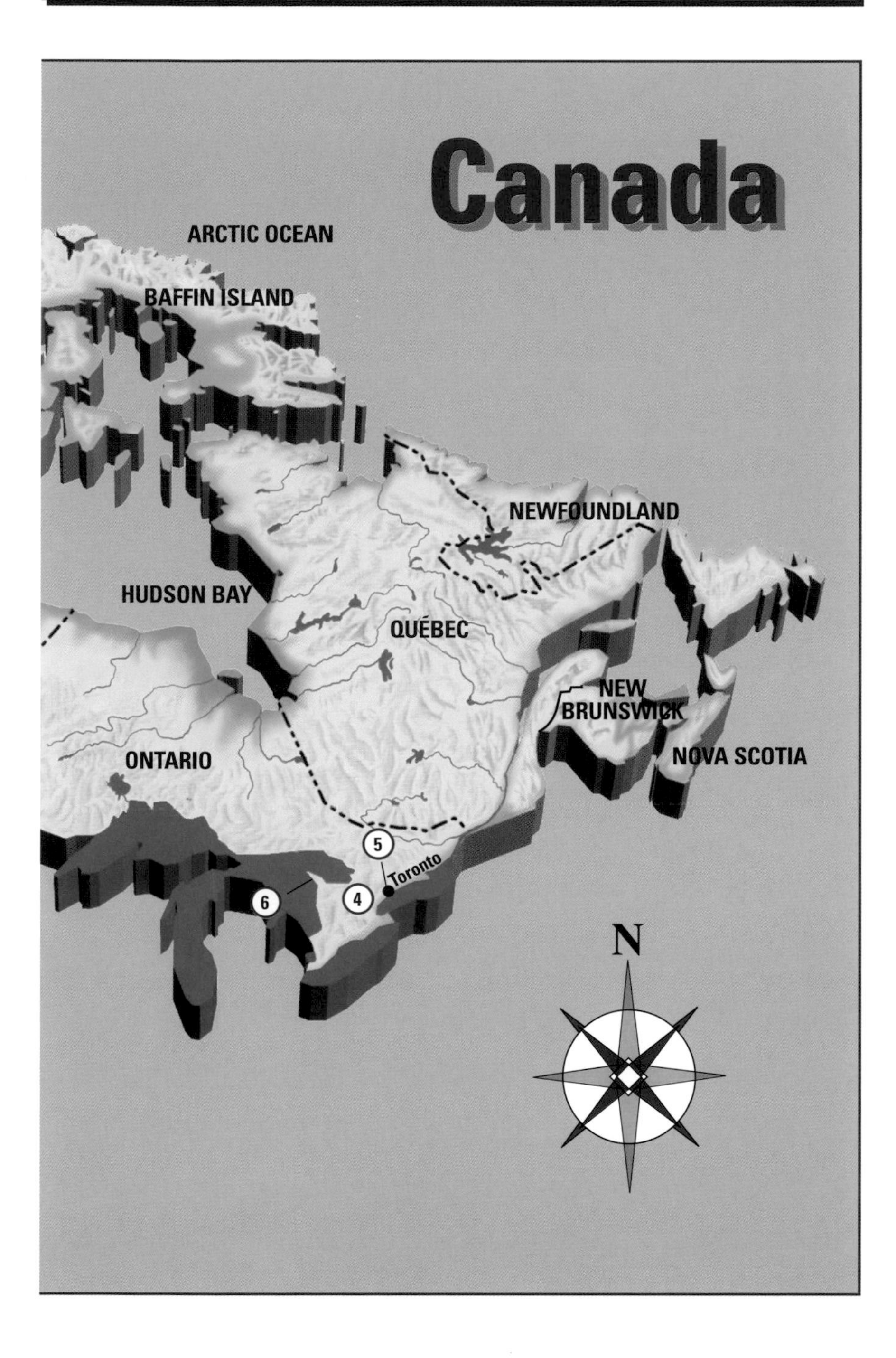
Canada
ARCTIC OCEAN
BAFFIN ISLAND
NEWFOUNDLAND
HUDSON BAY
QUÉBEC
NEW
BRUNSWICK
NOVA SCOTIA
ONTARIO
5
Toronto
4
6
N

The best crag for beginners and large groups is Rattlesnake Point, about a 45-minute drive southwest of Toronto. Routes are easily top-roped, but many are leadable. Expect a crowd on a nice weekend.

Lion's Head is one of the largest areas and faces into scenic Georgian Bay from the Bruce Peninsula. The routes at Lion's Head are excellent and most are bolted, but climbing there is serious. You must rappel to very exposed hanging belays to lead. If you lower down to top-rope a route, make sure it is within your capabilities or that you have a safe method for ascending the rope if you get stumped.

Classic Rock of The United Kingdom

Climbing history in the United Kingdom is rich and colorful, featuring a hearty collection of scary tales involving difficult moves on steep rock with little protection. Before the turn of the century, British climbers used their local rock as a training ground for greater exploits in the European Alps. By the 1940s and '50s, however, rock climbing had become a sport in its own right. A visit to Britain can put you on routes that were first climbed 100 years ago. Here you can also work out on some of the most difficult modern test pieces.

England

You will not find the sustained heights of Yosemite's El Capitan in England, but countless crags and short walls dot the countryside with thousands of routes to select from. A dozen or so major crags lie within an hour's drive of Manchester or Sheffield. The guidebooks to the various rocks list over 10,000 established routes. You can challenge the best on steep, slippery limestone, or experience the high friction of classic British gritstone.

Wales

A visit to Wales will take you back to the medieval days of knights in armor and wet, misty crags covered with moss. Most of the primary climbing areas are within an hour's drive of the village of Llanberis. To the north are the 60- to 120-meter walls of Dinas Cromlech. At nearby Llanberis Pass you'll find the tallest rock in Britain, Clogwyn du'r Arddu, or "Cloggy." At Gogarth, the routes rise directly from the sea, and Pembroke, several hours to the south, offers bolted sport climbs. When weather is bad, as it often is, there are castles to explore.

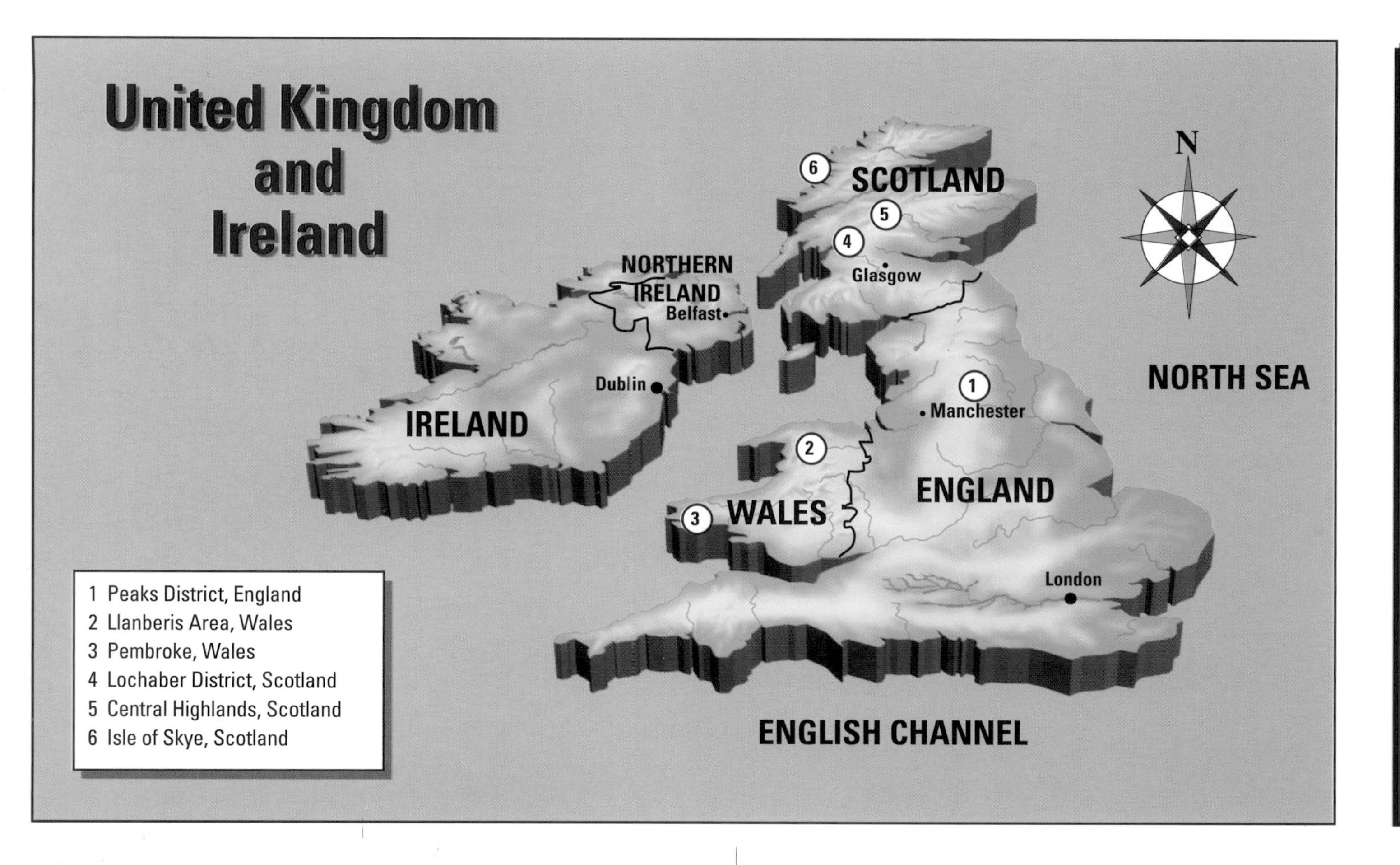
United Kingdom and Ireland
N
SCOTLAND
Glasgow
NORTHERN IRELAND
Belfast
Dublin
IRELAND
NORTH SEA
Manchester
WALES
ENGLAND
London
ENGLISH CHANNEL
1 Peaks District, England
2 Llanberis Area, Wales
3 Pembroke, Wales
4 Lochaber District, Scotland
5 Central Highlands, Scotland
6 Isle of Skye, Scotland

English gritstone at Brimham Rocks, North Yorkshire.

Scotland

When the rock is dry and the carnivorous insects are few (usually in spring and early summer), Scotland provides some beautiful routes into the sky. The coastal shores and interior hills provide countless crags and outcrops to explore. You'll find big-time exposure in Scotland, even on the easy routes. Check out *January Jigsaw* (5.4) on Buachaille Etive Mor in the Lochaber District, or the 260-meter *Minus One Direct* (5.7) on Ben Nevis, Scotland's highest mountain. Another long, easy route is the six-pitch slab route, *Ardverikie Wall*, on Binnein Shuas in the Central Highlands.

A visit to Scotland should include the magical Isle of Skye, a dramatic blend of rocky peaks and seascapes. Climbing at Skye dates back to the 1800s, yet new routes are still being choreographed.

Sron Na Ciche is a massive showpiece cliff of the southern Cuillin area. Halfway up the face is the Cioch, a wild rock protuberance worn slick by nearly a century of traffic. The area presents multipitch routes ranging from easy saunters up to 5.11.

A European Sampler 

Like Canada in North America, Europe has historically been a world-class center of Alpine mountaineering. While the glacier-clad peaks of the Alps still draw climbers from around the world, Europe has also become the center for sport rock climbing. The acceptance of ample bolt protection has enabled modern rock gymnasts to push the limits of human possibilities in relative safety. Most of the world's top competitive sport climbers are from Europe, or at least live and train there.

The concentration of high-quality rock over a relatively small geographic area makes Europe an attractive destination for vacationing climbers. On your requisite rest days, you will find countless villages and historical centers to explore, and the ocean is never far away.

Spain

Spain is the birthplace of the sticky rubber used for the soles of rock shoes, so it is no wonder that it offers a wealth of climbing. Just outside Madrid is the Regionale Park of Cuenta Alta of Manzanares, home to the huge, pink granite formations of La Pedriza. You can friction up the long exposed slabs of El Yelmo, or pull fully bolted sport routes on one of the boulders of the Rompeolas sector.

For sheer volume, the high area of Montserrat, or Sawtooth Mountain, offers countless spires of gray conglomerate. The mountain comes complete with a Benedictine monastery! You can drive to Montserrat or travel by train or bus from Barcelona, finishing with a cable-car ride to the monastery. There is climber-friendly camping at the monastery, which also has a grocery and restaurant.

French Destinations

France is a rock climber's paradise with good weather and rock everywhere. Although the French have dominated the world of competitive sport climbing, their home rock provides routes of all grades to be savored by everyone.

Two kilometers northeast of the village of Vingrau near France's southern border is an enjoyable escarpment of excellent gray limestone. The southern half of this chain of cliffs is primarily a bolted sport-climbing area with slab, face, and crack routes from 5.3 to 5.13. To the north towers the classic Petit Dru. The area receives much sunshine and can be extremely hot on summer afternoons. One drawback is the area's high incidence of theft, so do not leave valuables in your vehicle!

To the east is perhaps the sport-climbing center of Europe: the one-

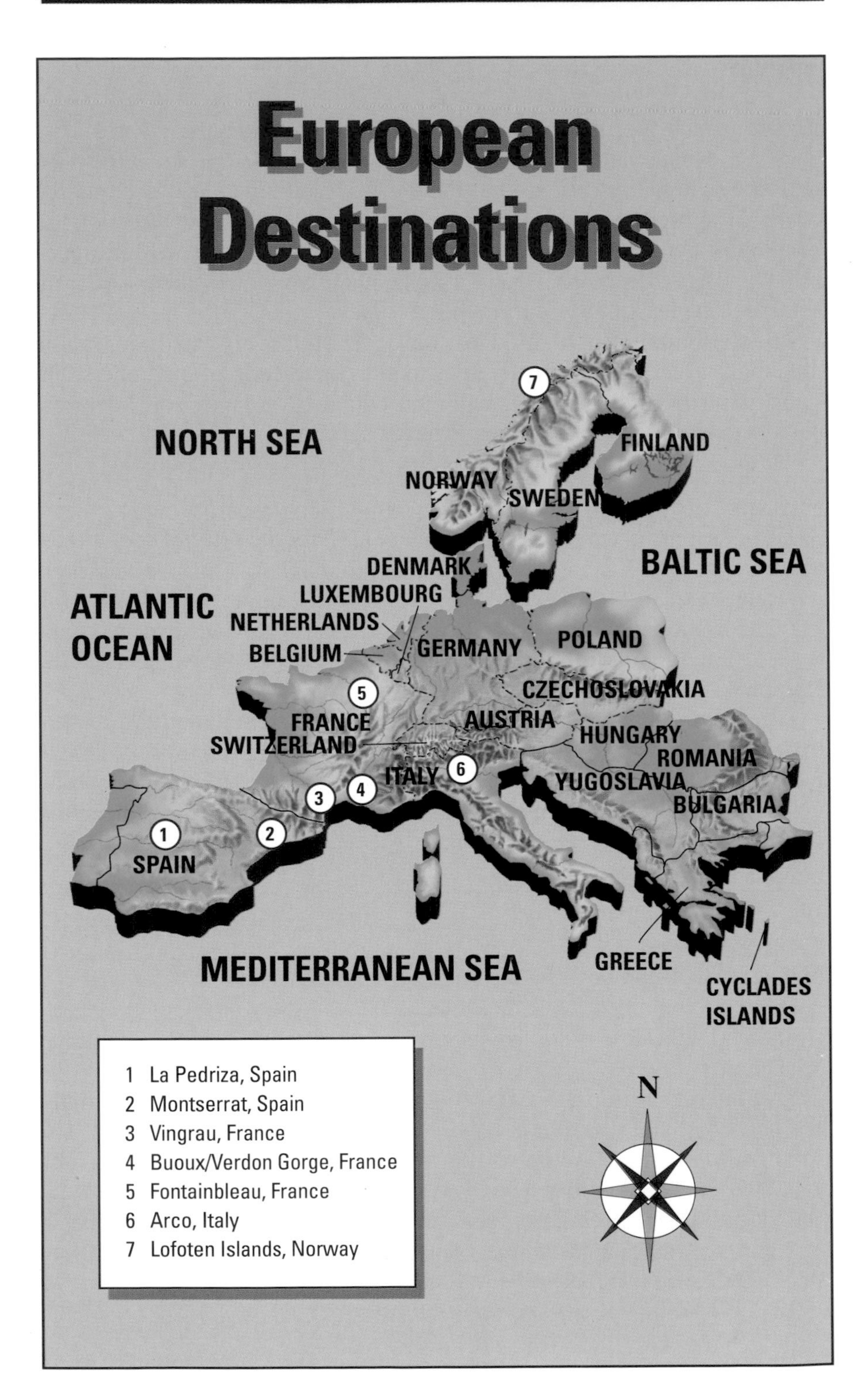
European Destinations
NORTH SEA
NORWAY
SWEDEN
FINLAND
DENMARK
BALTIC SEA
LUXEMBOURG
ATLANTIC OCEAN
NETHERLANDS
BELGIUM
GERMANY
POLAND
CZECHOSLOVAKIA
FRANCE
AUSTRIA
SWITZERLAND
HUNGARY
ROMANIA
ITALY
YUGOSLAVIA
BULGARIA
SPAIN
MEDITERRANEAN SEA
GREECE
CYCLADES ISLANDS
1 La Pedriza, Spain
2 Montserrat, Spain
3 Vingrau, France
4 Buoux/Verdon Gorge, France
5 Fontainbleau, France
6 Arco, Italy
7 Lofoten Islands, Norway
N

Fig. 5.7

kilometer-long cliff of Buoux. Here you will find hundreds of bolted routes (5.8-5.14) from 20 to 90 meters in length. Many routes here are at the leading edge of difficulty, and the beginner to intermediate climber will find little to enjoy.

A bit further east, leading into the blue water of Lake St. Croix, is the awe-inspiring Verdon Gorge, with 300-meter walls of white limestone. The Route des Cretes road passes above the gorge for a distance of about 14.5 kilometers. Most of the routes are understandably long and difficult. Access commonly involves serious multiple rappels from the rim.

Along the Autoroute de Soleil, A6, just a short distance from Paris, lies the beautiful Fontainbleau forest. With some 60 sub-areas, each containing hundreds of sandstone boulders, the "Bleau" has perhaps the best concentration of bouldering in the world. All routes are soloed, but most offer soft, sandy landings for the jump off.

One of the largest concentrations of problems is at L'Elephant, so named after the appearance of the first boulder encountered as you reach the rocks. Here you will find over 400 routes ranging in difficulty from 5.2 to hard 5.11. There are five main circuits, which are color coded and marked according to difficulty.

Camping in the forest or among the boulders is not allowed, but established campgrounds and lodgings are nearby. For roped sport climbing, the nearby areas of Le Parc and Le Saussois are pleasant options. The best seasons for climbing in the Fountainbleau are spring and autumn. November through March tend to be very wet months.

Pull-ups and Pizza in Italy

If well protected sport climbing interests you, the routes in several areas near the town of Arco, in northern Italy, are particularly user-friendly. With park-like settings and bomber bolts and anchors, you can crank to your heart's (or forearms') content. After you get your fill of pulling the overhangs of Massone, or dancing technical steps at Nago, sample some great Italian food as you recount the day's adventures.

Lofoten Islands, Norway

One guidebook refers to this area, 200 kilometers north of the Arctic Circle, as "the Magic Islands." Indeed they are, with enchanting beauty and perfect granite as well. Once in Norway, various combinations of trains, buses, and ferries can get you to the islands where all major towns are connected via bus routes. Campsites are abundant in Lofoten.

The Nord Norsk Klatreskole (climbing school) in Henningsvaer is the place to obtain local information. This is also the locale of the Klatrekafe'en, or *Climbing Cafe*, where you can meet potential climbing partners.

The routes in the Lofoten Islands are traditional-style adventures. Bring a full rack of gear and 50-meter ropes, as the pitches and rappels are long. June through August is the time to come to Lofoten, but don't come without warm clothes even during the summer.

Climbing Down Under 

The best rock in Australia is concentrated in the south between Sydney and Melbourne. Tasmania also offers some good rock along the coast. Mount Arapiles holds perhaps the best known Australian rock, with over 2,000 routes on hard sandstone. A good selection of moderate routes plus plenty of severe crankers will keep everyone entertained for days at this primarily traditional lead climbing area.

Close to Sydney are the Blue Mountains, with their many bolted routes and sandstone that is rough and abrasive to the fingertips. Visiting the nearby villages and bakeries is fun on off-days. Campsites are readily available near each climbing area. You can find suitable weather just about year-round, but spring and fall are best. Summers (January and February) can get hot.

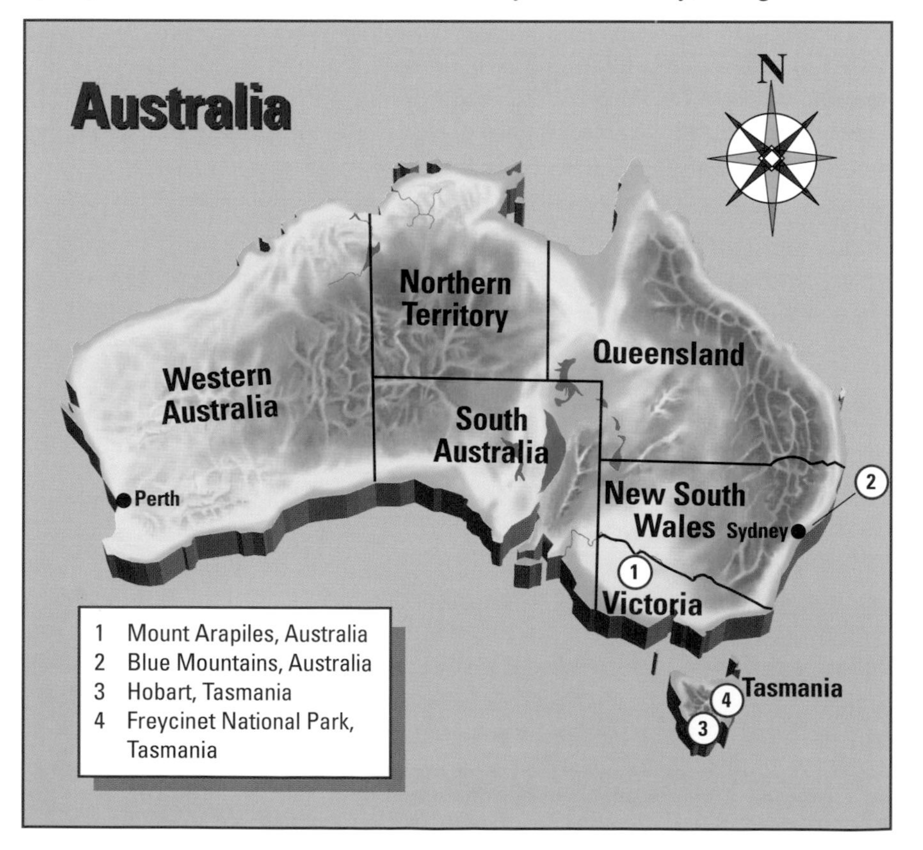

Tasmania has several appealing areas along its northern and eastern shorelines. The capital of Hobart is host to the 1.6 kilometer-long band of brown limestone known as the *Organ Pipes* and several in-town quarries with bolted sport routes. Freycinet National Park is up the coast from Hobart a bit, on a beautiful peninsula. There are crack climbs at Bluestone Bay and smooth runout slabs at the Hazards.

Other Summits

You can climb just about anywhere. Whether you are on vacation or a business trip, or attending an international conference, pack your rock shoes and some gear!

Additional areas of note are the basaltic crags of the Izu Peninsula of Japan and Lion Rock near Hong Kong. The Todra Gorge of Morocco contains sport routes on limestone, while many routes, traditional and sport, abound in the vicinity of Cape Town, South Africa. While most noted for Alpine mountaineering, countries along the Andes region of South America offer a considerable amount of pure rock climbing as well.

Check with one of the guidebook sources listed in the Appendix for references to a particular country. The popular rock-climbing and mountaineering magazines often publish articles and mini-guides to choice areas around the world.

6

PURSUING CLIMBING FURTHER

Once you have mastered the basics and are honing your technique and expertise on the rocks, you may develop an interest in climbing other mediums, such as ice and snow, or venturing into the realm of high mountains. You may also wish to test your skills in organized rock-climbing competitions.

It is well beyond the scope of this book to present comprehensive coverage of ice and snow climbing or mountaineering. The structured training necessary to become a world-class competitor is complex and best presented at length. References on these extensions of the sport of rock climbing are provided in the appendix. This chapter gives you a basic description of these activities.

Competitive Sport Climbing

I was first exposed to competition climbing as a spectator at an International World Cup event. I considered myself primarily a mountaineer, who enjoyed the "freedom of the hills," and was skeptical about climbing artificially designed routes under a set of rules. It did not take long for the excitement of the event and the tremendous talent of the athletes to win more than a bit of my respect. Since then, I have even found myself waiting my turn on the wall at local competitions.

Organized climbing competitions differ a bit from area to area, but most have settled on an *on-sight difficulty* format. Competitors are judged on how far they can progress over a pre-set route without any prior information on or examination of the route.

There are usually one or more elimination rounds, then the top scorers climb a new, more difficult route for the finals. If a climber falls, that's it; her highest point is identified and a score calculated.

The proliferation of modular indoor walls has benefited competitions, because unique routes may be designed that have never before been attempted. Artificial walls provide standardized, weatherproof conditions for all competitors, and facilitate spectator viewing as well.

A yearly, multiple-event World Cup circuit was launched in the late 1980s that determines individual event winners and overall male and female series champions. However, you don't have to schedule a round-the-world tour to give competition climbing a try. Most indoor climbing walls and gyms offer some type of competitive event each year. Local clubs sometimes host outdoor bouldering contests, which bring the climbing community together for a day of fun in the sun. Local contests usually have some type of ability and age groupings for the awards. Stores that carry climbing gear, indoor walls and gyms, and magazines are good sources of information about upcoming events.

Although you may feel some anxiety as you await your turn in your first climbing competition, you will likely find that the challenge, social scene, and just plain fun eventually outweigh the stress. Here are a few tips that may help you prepare for and survive your first on-sight competition:

- If possible, get in some practice time at the site. Become familiar with the holds and how they can be used. The course setter will change everything around, and probably will add some unfamiliar holds, but being comfortable with the facility will help.
- When the competition employs an isolation area, bring something to munch on, a water bottle, and a good book or a Walkman.

A World Cup sport climbing competition at Snowbird, Utah.

- Warm up thoroughly before going out to climb. I like to get in 15 to 20 minutes of easy jogging or other aerobic exercise to ease the jitters, followed by an extended stretching sequence. If a bouldering wall is available, I will work through several short sequences that involve upward, downward, and lateral moves.
- Know the specific rules of the contest. Are the route boundaries clearly marked? Can you attempt the route again after a fall, or is it one fall and out? Is there a time limit?
- Check out the safety procedures carefully. Contact the person who will be belaying you and assure that your communication signals are clear.

Remember, the challenge is not you against the other climbers. Rather, you want to see how well you can solve the puzzle (the route) that is presented—and have some fun along the way.

Ice Climbing

When the crags are cold and mantled by snow and the indoor gyms get crowded, some rock climbers still seek the joy and excitement of climbing in the outdoors. Winter turns the waterfalls and seepages of summer into a variety of frozen pillars, curtains, and hanging icicles, with characteristics as varied as rock types.

Ice climbing shares many similarities with rock climbing. You may boulder, top-rope, or lead routes, and the basic belay techniques are the same. There are differences, however, that are critical to your safety and enjoyment of this variant of the climbing game. Before you gear up for an ascent of ice, you should get some expert instruction.

Much of the uniqueness in ice climbing comes from the specialized equipment employed. *Crampons*, sharp, spiked, metal frames, are strapped to the soles of the climber's boots to provide foot purchase. Using both arms, hand-held ice-axes are swung in an arc into the ice above. Protection for leading comes from tubular ice screws, which are turned or hammered into the ice and connected to the rope with a quickdraw.

It is the medium—the ice—and the setting that draw climbers to this game. The variable nature of frozen water, from the Styrofoam-like quality of perfect glacier ice to the brittle hardness of a January waterfall, provides an array of challenging situations. The subtle colors within the ice and the quiet of winter heighten the allure of the ice-climbing experience.

© Glenn Randall

Ice climbing in the Rocky Mountains.

Alpine Mountaineering

On the high mountains it all comes together. You step off the trail and head cross-country with map and compass to locate your chosen peak. You establish camp on a flat rock outcrop, safe from the hazards of rockfall and snow avalanche, where you can visually scout the mountain for the best route.

You rise before dawn and make a quick, warm breakfast to break the chill. Soon, crampons are affixed to boots and you settle into the rhythm of the approach up the glacier. The sun breaks the horizon as the slope steepens, the rays glittering gold and pink off the edges of deep crevasses in the ice. These dark chambers must be safely negotiated while you keep watch for others that may be hidden beneath the snow. Your roped team of climbers must coordinate movement and speed to progress efficiently.

The glacier gives way to a rib of broken rock. You remove your crampons to allow good friction on the blocks above. You are careful not to loosen rocks that could fall on the climbers below. A difficult section requires you to set up an anchor and belay. You edge and smear; crimp and jam; chimney and stem.

Always you are searching the way ahead for the best route. You must balance the safety of solid terrain and lots of protection anchors with the safety of moving fast to avoid getting caught in a sudden storm or facing dangerous avalanche conditions in the heat of the afternoon.

Finally, the summit! You are contented to have negotiated the mountain's puzzles. The view is inspiring and the air invigorating. However, this is only

Topping the Roman Wall on Mt. Baker, a giant volcano in the North Cascades Range.

the halfway point. A careful descent must be executed before the real celebration can begin.

Descending may involve careful downclimbing or complicated rappels. You must renegotiate the glacier, in which new crevasses have opened since the early morning hours. You are tired, physically and mentally, but must still execute with the same perfection that got you safely to the summit. Finally, your camp is in sight, and you look forward to concocting a hot drink as alpenglow settles over the mountain.

There is nothing quite like a successful technical ascent of a high mountain. Some peaks offer pure rock routes, but others also demand ice- and snow-climbing skills. The successful integration of such skills is a rewarding experience.

The risks of Alpine mountaineering are considerably higher than those you are exposed to on a bolted sport route at an established rock crag. Problems with weather, loose rock, avalanche, and the difficulty of rescue in a remote, rugged area can be serious. These risks are not always predictable; you must be able to avoid mistakes when fatigued and under duress. Judgment becomes a major factor in surviving to climb again, and this is impossible to learn from a book.

SAFETY TIP

Before you venture onto the big peaks, get some specialized instruction in the field and apprentice with partners you can trust. The resources listed in the appendix will help you locate a school or guide service in your area.

Closing Thoughts

For many, rock climbing has become not only a challenging activity, but a source of joy. The famous French mountain guide, Gaston Rebuffat, perhaps said it best:

"To climb smoothly, between sky and earth, in a succession of precise, efficient movements, induces an inner peace and even a mood of gaiety . . . . A difficulty constitutes a question; the movements which resolve it are the reply. This is the intimate pleasure of communicating with the mountain . . . with its substance, as an artist communicates with the wood, stone, or iron. . . . Both the climbing and the feeling become like spring water, which is born of the earth and flows gently embracing its banks." (*On Ice and Snow and Rock*, 1971)

My seasons of climbing have given me countless joys and not a few exciting moments. The partners with whom I have shared the rope have become friends for life, and our reminiscences are priceless. I hope that climbing will provide you with much of the same. Whether you are interested in bouldering, top-roping, or leading, the rock awaits you. Happy climbing!

APPENDIX
FOR MORE INFORMATION

Organizations

Rock-climbing and mountaineering organizations are valuable sources of information concerning national and regional climbing clubs, schools, and good places to climb. The American Mountain Guides Association is a good contact for locating rock-climbing schools and guide services for a particular area.

Access Committee
Alpine Club of Canada
35 Front St. E.
Toronto, Ontario M5E 1B3
Canada

Access Fund
P.O. Box 17010
Boulder, CO 80308
U.S.A.
(303) 545-6772

Alpine Club of Canada
P.O. Box 1026
Banff, Alberta TOL 0C0
Canada

American Alpine Club
710 Tenth St., Suite 100
Golden, CO 80401
U.S.A.
(303) 384-0110 / Fax (303) 384-0111

American Mountain Guides Association
710 Kent Street, Suite 101
Golden, CO 80401
U.S.A.
(303) 271-0984

American Sport Climbers Federation
125 West 96th Street
Suite #1D
New York, NY 10025
U.S.A.

British Mountaineering Council
177/9 Burton Road
West Didsbury
Manchester M20 2BB
England
161-445-4747

Federation Francaise de la Montagne
20 bis Rue La Boetie
75008 Paris
France

Club Alpino Italiano
Via Ugo Foscolo 3
20121 Milano
Italy

National Centre for Mountaineering Activities
Plas y Brenin
Capel Curig
Gwynedd LL24 OET
North Wales

Norsk Tindeklub
P.O. Boks 1727
Vika
Oslo 1
Norway

Federacion Espanola de Montanismo
Alberto Aguilera 3-4°
Madrid 15
Spain

Books

Climbing Anchors, by John Long. Evergreen, Colorado: Chockstone Press, Inc., 1993.

Climbing Rock and Ice, by Jerry Cinnamon. Blue Ridge Summit, Pennsylvania: Ragged Mountain Press, 1994.

How To Rock Climb! (2nd ed.), by John Long. Evergreen, Colorado: Chockstone Press, Inc., 1993.

Mountaineering: The Freedom of The Hills (5th ed.), Don Graydon (Ed.). Seattle, Washington: The Mountaineers, 1992.

Performance Rock Climbing, by Dale Goddard and Udo Neumann. Mechanicsburg, Pennsylvania: Stackpole Books, 1993.

Guidebooks

Practically every established climbing area offers a written guidebook, if only a stapled collection of photocopied sketches of the routes. Published guidebooks are usually available at local climbing shops or via mail order from one of the following sources.

Backcountry Bookstore
Box 6235-CL
Lynnwood, WA 98036
U.S.A.

Chessler Books
P.O. Box 399
Kittredge, CO 80457
U.S.A.
(800) 654-8502 or (303) 670-0093

J. P. Books
Box 10884
Portland, OR 97210
U.S.A.
(503) 227-3308

The Second Step
York Arcade
80 Islington High Street
Camden Passage
London N1 8EQ
England
171 359 6412

Periodicals

Climbing journals and magazines are usually published monthly or quarterly throughout the year. Periodicals provide you with articles on technique, equipment reviews, and mini-guides to specific areas. They also are great references for mail-order suppliers of equipment and gear.

Climber and Hillwalker
Outram Magazines
Plaza Tower
East Kilbride
Glasgow G74 1LW
Scotland

Climbing
1101 Village Road, Suite LL-1-B
Carbondale, CO 81623
U.S.A.
(303) 963-9449 / Fax (303) 963-9442

Rock & Ice
P.O. Box 3595
Boulder, CO 80307
U.S.A.
(303) 499-8410 / Fax (303) 499-4131

Videos

Many scenic and entertaining rock-climbing videotapes are available from mountaineering/rock-climbing specialty shops and bookstores. Not all of these are instructional, however. Here is a partial list of videos that provide historical and instructional information.

Basic Rock Climbing
Vertical Adventures Productions
3200 Wilshire Blvd., Suite 1207
Los Angeles, CA 90010
U.S.A.

The Art of Leading
Chockstone Productions
526 Franklin Street
Denver, CO 80218
U.S.A.

Moving Over Stone and *Moving Over Stone II*
Range of Light Productions
P.O. Box 2906
Mammoth Lakes, CA 93546
U.S.A.

Performance Rock Climbing—The Video
1478 East Logan
Salt Lake City, UT 84105
U.S.A.

ROCK CLIMBING LINGO

Although you can develop your climbing skills through silent bouldering, in order to reap the social advantages of the sport, and to be able to communicate in the many areas you will visit, you need to become somewhat literate in rock-climbing lingo.

aid—An abbreviation for the use of artificial aids to support one's body weight or assist in progress up the rock. Also the style of Class 6, or artificial, climbing.

barndoor—The effect of an unbalanced position on the rock that causes your body to swing off the rock like a barndoor.

belay—The system for, or act of, managing the rope to protect the climber.

bell ringer—A fall off to the side of an upper anchor point that, as the rope becomes tight, produces a wild series of swings, much like a ringing bell.

beta—Specific verbal or written information about a given climbing route's holds or moves.

biner—Short for carabiner. Gated aluminum snap-links that are used to connect various components of the climbing system.

bomber—Outstanding; may be used to describe the quality of protection, anchors for a route, or a specific hold.

cam—An artificial anchor device employing a curved shape that tends to wedge the device tighter in the rock when loaded by force.

clean—To remove the intermediate anchors, or pro, placed during a lead climb.

comp—An organized sport-climbing competition.

crater—To fall and hit the ground.

crimper—A small, sometimes sharp, hold that requires you to hyperextend the first knuckles of your fingers.

crux—The most difficult move or series of moves on a specific pitch or route.

exposure—A characteristic of a climbing route or position that indicates extreme steepness or distance from level ground.

fixed pro—Protection gear that is permanently left in the rock.

free—A style of climbing that does not rely on artificial aid during the ascent. Also the act of climbing a former Class 6 aid climb without artificial aids.

gripped—Scared to the point of being unable to release holds on the rock and thus to proceed. A complete erasure of all mojo.

hangdog—To rest by hanging on the rope between attempts to complete a move or sequence of moves. An ascent which includes hangdogging is not considered a completely free ascent.

lead—To climb first on a route, placing intermediate anchors to which the rope is attached.

lieback—A move that involves creating counterpressure to make the feet stick by lying back and pulling with the hands while the feet press into the rock. Very strenuous.

mojo—A state of mind or psyche that enables one to overcome extreme physical or mental difficulties in climbing. Mojo is a good thing most of the time, but it has led some climbers into foolishness.

monodoight—A small pocket in the rock that will accept only one finger.

natural gear—Protection gear that you put in place during a lead.

pitch—The distance between belay points on a route or the number of belay points necessary to complete a long route (as in three-pitch).

pro—An abbreviated expression for protection, or intermediate anchors. Also used as a generic term for the gear used to establish anchors.

problem—A generic term for a perplexing or difficult section of climbing.

pumped—A state of rigor in the forearm muscles, which grow engorged with blood as a result of extreme effort during a climb. Associated with fatigue and an inability to grasp holds.

quickdraw—A short loop of sewn webbing into which two carabiners are clipped.

runner—A tied or sewn loop of webbing used to connect various components of the anchor systems.

runout—Refers to a particularly long section of climbing between anchors.

screamer—A fall during which the involved climber emits some type of scream, yelp, or other audible vocalization.

second—The climber who ascends after the leader, with a belay from above. The second will usually clean the protection.

sequence—A specific series of moves that are necessary for success on a route.

sewing-machine leg—A phenomenon that involves a climber's leg shaking involuntarily. Usually caused by maintaining a set position for an extended period, particularly with the heel higher than the toe.

thin— Lacking distinct holds or textures; can refer to a specific hold or an entire route.

whipper—A long leader fall, or a fall that occurs with slack in the rope, resulting in the climber experiencing a whip-like snap as the rope comes taut.

yo-yo—To climb up a bit, place protection, and get lowered to the ground; then climb up again, place more protection, get lowered, and so on.

zipper—To rip out a succession of protection placements during a fall.

INDEX

Note: Page numbers in italics refer to illustrations. Page numbers in boldface refer to glossary entries.

ACKNOWLEDGMENT

If Vera T. Watts had said, "You better stay off those rocks!", I might have listened, and there would have been no book. But Mom never did say that. If Annette and Salem had not sauntered the hills with me, I might have spent weekends mowing the lawn and had no feel for footholds and handholds or high summits. But my family understood, and we all learned the joys of fresh air high among the crags. If my climbing partners had not given solid belays when the crux undercling broke off at Smith, when I got pumped and missed the critical bolt clip in the Needles, or when . . . , there would have been little to tell. But those with whom I have shared the rope held the belays, and our past and future visions weave a tapestry for the telling. Thanks to all of these!

ABOUT THE AUTHOR

© Miles Prahl

Phil Watts has instructed hundreds of rock climbers through various outdoor programs and university courses.

Introduced to rock climbing in 1979, Phil since then has completed many outdoor adventure courses, including an 8-day Technical Rock Climbing course at the Canadian Outward Bound Mountain School, a 31-day North Cascades Mountaineering course at the National Outdoor Leadership School, an 8-day Technical Ice Climbing course at the American Alpine Institute. He has extensive climbing experience on many surfaces, including granite, sandstone, basalt, and other rock types.

After earning both a bachelor's degree in health and physical education (1973) and a master's degree in physical education from East Carolina University, Greenville, North Carolina, Phil completed a PhD in exercise physiology (1980) from the University of Maryland, College Park. Since 1983 his research has focused on mountaineering and rock climbing.

Phil has developed and taught his own outdoor adventure programs and courses and presented several workshops and colloquiums on the physiological aspects of rock climbing. His work has appeared in such publications as the *Journal of Sports Sciences*, the *Journal of Sports Medicine and Physical Fitness*, *Summit*, and *Rock & Ice*.

Phil resides in Marquette, Michigan where local climbers have even named a crag after him—Phil's Hill. He's an avid cross-country skiing competitor and enjoys hiking and camping with his wife, Annette, and their daughter, Salem.

Other books in the
Outdoor Pursuits Series
OUTDOOR PURSUITS SERIES
WALKING
OUTDOOR PURSUITS SERIES
SNOWSHOEING
OUTDOOR PURSUITS SERIES
HIKING AND BACKPACKING
ERIC SEABORG • ELLEN DUDLEY
OUTDOOR PURSUITS SERIES
CANOEING
OUTDOOR PURSUITS SERIES
WINDSURFING
OUTDOOR PURSUITS SERIES
SNOW-BOARDING
ROB REICHENFELD • ANNA BRUECHERT
OUTDOOR PURSUITS SERIES
MOUNTAIN BIKING
DON DAVIS • DAVE CARTER
OUTDOOR PURSUITS SERIES
Whitewater and Sea
KAYAKING
KENT FORD
Other titles in the Outdoor Pursuits Series:
• Orienteering
(Available Fall 1996)
To request more information or to place your order, U.S. customers call TOLL-FREE 1-800-747-4457.
Customers outside the U.S. use appropriate telephone number/address shown in the front of this book.
Human Kinetics
The Premier Publisher for Sports & Fitness
2335